TWENTIETH CENTURY INTERPRETATIONS

OF

SONS AND LOVERS

A Collection of Critical Essays

Edited by

JUDITH FARR

Prentice-Hall, Inc. A SPECTRUM BOOK *Englewood Cliffs, N. J.*

Quotations from *Sons and Lovers* by D. H. Lawrence used by permission of The Viking Press, Inc. and Laurence Pollinger, Ltd.

Current printing (last number):

10   9   8   7   6   5   4   3   2   1

PRENTICE-HALL INTERNATIONAL, INC. (*London*)
PRENTICE-HALL OF AUSTRALIA, PTY. LTD. (*Sydney*)
PRENTICE-HALL OF CANADA, LTD. (*Toronto*)
PRENTICE-HALL OF INDIA PRIVATE LIMITED (*New Delhi*)
PRENTICE-HALL OF JAPAN, INC. (*Tokyo*)

Contents

TWENTIETH CENTURY
INTERPRETATIONS
OF
SONS AND LOVERS

Introduction[1]

When David Herbert Lawrence died of tuberculosis in 1930 at Vence, France, he was forty-four years old, the author of thirteen novels and numerous short stories, poems, plays, travel books, and articles. His Coleridgean dream of "Rananim," an ideal community in which to live, had taken him to Germany, Italy, Australia, Mexico, New Mexico, Switzerland, and France—far from the Nottinghamshire mining village of his birth that he describes in *Sons and Lovers*. His life, he said, had been a "savage enough pilgrimage." Acclaimed as a great writer, reviled as a pornographer, adulated but misrepresented by sexual cultists, worshipped as a prophet of Freudianism and anarchsim, he was loved by his wife and friends as a man of rare charity and deplored by Katherine Mansfield as "filthy," "a reptile," by Bertrand Russell as "a positive force for evil." The "new" novels that Lawrence considered his contribution to English letters, novels like *The Rainbow* (his favorite) and *Women in Love,* had encountered public outrage and critical shrugs. During a career, however, in which few could agree either upon his character as a man or his qualities as an artist, Lawrence was often commended or excused because he was the author of *Sons and Lovers.*

D. H. Lawrence was born on September 11, 1885, in the Midlands mining town of Eastwood to the miner Arthur Lawrence and his wife, Lydia Beardsall Lawrence. Like his four brothers and sisters, "Bert" Lawrence was devoted to their prudent, energetic mother who sometimes wrote verse and who proudly traced her lineage to lace manufacturers and to the hymn-writer, John Newton; but he disliked his working-class father. Some Lawrence acquaintants point out that the father was a good provider, whose homes at the Breach (the "Bottoms" of *Sons and Lovers*) and later, on Walker Street ("Scargill Street"), were comfortable and who sent each of his children to school or college. The children themselves, however, seem on the whole to have agreed with their famous brother that Arthur Lawrence's drinking and blustering taught his family "horror." When Bert Lawrence finished school, he worked briefly as a surgical appliances clerk, then prepared at Nottingham University to be a teacher. Keenly fond of his "home valley," whose mines gave way to the

[1] I owe thanks to my husband, George F. Farr, Jr., for redemptive criticism of this essay in its stages.

Annesley woods where Byron had walked with Mary Chaworth, Lawrence was pained to be assigned a school in far-off Croydon. There, too frail and too original to enjoy such hard teaching, he began his first novels. After his mother's death in 1910, with the encouragement of his wife Frieda, Lawrence gave up teaching altogether for writing and travelling. For the most part he lived abroad in Italy, France, and New Mexico. Publishing voluminously, he evolved a sexual philosophy and a lyrical style that attracted hosannas, scorn, and police censure. No longer pale "Bert," he had become "Lorenzo," the "magical D. H. Lawrence." At his death, doctors marvelled that his ruined lungs had allowed him such vital industry. His literary supporters included William Butler Yeats and E. M. Forster, who was mocked by T. S. Eliot for declaring Lawrence "the greatest imaginative novelist of [his] generation." When his more demonstrative admirers tried to steal his body from its tomb in Taos, New Mexico, his widow was forced to rebury him in a slab of concrete. Despite the controversial reputation of his later books, it had become the fashion by 1928 for most students to read *Sons and Lovers:* one of two best-selling novels of that year on The Modern Library List.

Lawrence produced three major versions of *Sons and Lovers,* the novel he called his first "great book." *Paul Morel,* as the two early drafts are known, was begun in 1910 in Croydon, England, shortly before his mother died of cancer and during his tormented service as schoolmaster to miners' sons. Writing to Helen Corke, a fellow teacher, that in his aridity and grief "the one beautiful and generous adventure left seemed to be death," he subsequently enthused to her and others about his "colliery novel": "Glory, you should see it! The British public will stone me if it ever catches sight [of it]." *Paul Morel* was to be more faithfully autobiographical than *The White Peacock* or *The Trespasser,* which had preceded it. Lawrence described it in letters as "autobiography" and declared later that those interested in him should "read *Sons and Lovers,* the first part is all autobiography."

The interval spent in writing *Paul Morel* was crucial for the nervous, bronchitic young man of twenty-six. Hating his father, job, and surroundings and tempted by the cordial reception of his first books to escape to an artist's life abroad, he was struggling to accept the loss of his mother, whom he admitted having loved "almost with a husband and wife love" and who had had "his soul" so that "nobody [could] have it again." *Paul Morel* and the quixotic events surrounding it seemed an exorcism. Lawrence suddenly engaged himself to an old school-mate, Louie Burrows, on a train speeding through the Midlands. A few days later he announced it ("I never meant to. But she accepted me . . .") to Jessie Chambers, the farm-girl who had, as he later put it, "roused him to critical and creative consciousness" and who expected to be his wife.

The history of Jessie's involvement with *Sons and Lovers,* like Helen Corke's with *The Trespasser* or Mollie Skinner's with *The Boy in the Bush,* is a story in itself; and Lawrence, who insisted in a preface to his *Collected Poems* that even the best art "needs the penumbra of its own time and place and circumstance to make it full and whole," openly invited comparison of this story with that of Miriam Leivers in the book. "Bert" Lawrence—like his hero Paul Morel, the delicate son of a scarcely literate miner and the school-mistress daughter of a burgher—began visiting Jessie's farm at Greasley Haggs when he was fifteen. Jessie was then a sensitive repressed girl of fourteen, ardent for books, Wesleyanism, and nature. They grew up together, talking first about flowers and *Little Women,* then finally, as Ford Madox Ford marvelled, about "Nietzsche and Wagner and Leopardi and Flaubert and Karl Marx and Darwin." (Ford also recalled their separation when Lawrence wearied of a relationship that he later mocked as "sex in the head.") It was Jessie who submitted Lawrence's verse to Ford's *English Review* and who served him as critic and confidante in the manner of certain characters in his early fiction. Even after his engagement, she was not dismissed as confidante. In 1911, he sent her two-thirds of the first version of *Paul Morel.* Its plot was substantially the same as it would be in *Sons and Lovers.*[2] Yet it struck Jessie as "story-bookish" and "strain[ed]." She urged him to "write the whole story again, and keep it true to life," offering for raw material her own account of their adolescence.[3] In his quest for precise (and particularly the feminine) emotional nuance, Lawrence was often to accept such help. He welcomed Jessie's suggestion and later used her notes to alter and improve some scenes between Paul and Miriam. But the vivid draft of the near-complete *Paul Morel* shocked and alienated Jessie. She had hoped that the exercise of writing might destroy Lawrence's passion for his mother who, as "virgin" and "bride," haunted his poems. Instead, she considered his "bondage" to Lydia Lawrence "glorified and made absolute" in *Paul Morel.* A few months later, after reading the final proofs of *Sons and Lovers,* forwarded to her by an estranged Lawrence who was already expatriate, newly in love, and sure that his poetic "daimon" had rights superior to hers, she told Helen Corke that "the 'Miriam' part of the novel is a slander, a fearful treachery . . . I believe . . . that David's mind is . . . unhinged." Lawrence made lifelong ripostes to her de-

---

[2] Except, significantly, that Lawrence treated Walter Morel more severely, having him kill Paul's brother, go to jail, and die upon release. (For a careful account of the differences among the texts, see Harry T. Moore's essay, "The Genesis [of *Sons and Lovers*] as Revealed in the Miriam Papers," in *The Life and Works of D. H. Lawrence* (New York: Twayne Publishers, 1951), pp. 365–87.

[3] Jessie Chambers, *D. H. Lawrence, A Personal Record* (London: Jonathan Cape, Ltd., 1935), pp. 190–92.

nial that they were lovers, some—like a suppressed poem "Ah, Muriel!"
—implying that she was right,[4] others abusing her for hypocrisy or false
shame. Long after Jessie had destroyed her painful romance, *The
Rathe Primrose* (or *Eunice Temple*), married a schoolmaster, and
become a quiet, if embittered, Marxist, Lawrence continued to pun-
ish her with an artist's compliment, making her the prototype of his
Hermiones, Elsas, and Mrs. Pinnegars: of the cleverly spiritual, asexual
woman, "adorned" but "null in the flesh."

A different woman assisted in the three-months-long translation of
Paul Morel into *Sons and Lovers*, for during May, 1912, Lawrence
eloped with Frieda von Richthofen Weekley, a German baroness,
mother of three and wife of his former French professor. As the couple
traveled through Germany, Austria, and Italy, in poverty amid persim-
mons and roses, *Paul Morel* was "licked . . . into form" and newly
titled. Next it was sent for pruning to Edward Garnett of Duckworth.
(Lawrence's earlier publisher, William Heinemann, had refused it,
either in private pique or because, as Lawrence reported him saying,
it was "the dirtiest book he had ever read.") Ample, humorous Frieda
combined the physical qualities of Lawrence's "Claras"—Louie Burrows, suffragette Alice Dax, and an unnamed Eastwood mistress—with
an aristocratic lineage that intrigued Lawrence and would, he thought,
have mollified his mother. Like Jessie, she claimed to have supplied
specifically "female bits" of *Sons and Lovers;* and, perhaps before the
book's completion, she introduced Lawrence to the theories of Freud.[5]
With *Sons and Lovers* done, Lawrence announced that he would never
work again in so "sensational" a mode. He wrote the "Look! We
Have Come Through" poems to chronicle the achievement of serenity
with Frieda and pronounced his early life closed.

In fact, however, it was not closed, either as trauma or as the central
mythos into which the artist Lawrence gradually shaped it. For Lawrence the man, his boyhood delights and agonies stayed vivid. Writing
of "Miriam"'s farm to Jessie Chambers' brother David in 1928, his
letter glowed: "Whatever else I am, I am somewhere still the same

---

[4] I have many prayers to say
   If I string the planets and the beady stars
   Into a glistening rosary,
   'Twill not be too many prayers to say.

   For I have injured you. . . .

[5] Frederick J. Hoffman in "Lawrence's Quarrel with Freud" (Harry T. Moore and
Frederick J. Hoffman, eds., *The Achievement of D. H. Lawrence*, Norman, Oklahoma: University of Oklahoma Press, 1953, pp. 106–27) quotes a letter sent him by
Frieda Lawrence Ravagli in 1942 which states that "Lawrence knew about Freud
before he wrote the final draft of *Sons and Lovers*." Mrs. Ravagli could not recall
"whether he had read Freud or heard of him before [she met Lawrence] in 1912";
but said they argued together about Freud's doctrines, which Lawrence, like Joseph
Conrad, found "too limited and mechanical."

Bert who rushed with such joy to the Haggs." For Lawrence the writer, the experience behind *Sons and Lovers* served as poetic matrix and paradigm. The novelist who gives voice to the rage of Lady Chatterley's gamekeeper at a boyhood sweetheart; the essayist who fulminates against the murder of a child's "warm, swift, sensual self" by aggressive "Parent Love"; the poet praising death, pansies, and Indians, and hating the middle class, machines, and egoistic lovemaking, are all the Lawrence who created Paul Morel, with his virginal and Oedipal anxieties, enamored of "night, and death, and stillness, and inaction," interested in primitive tribes, believing in the wholesomeness of flowers and the common people, convicted in the book itself of a caddish, angry, yet wistful sexuality. Lawrence's chief theme, which he summarized as "the relation between men and women," expresses itself in *Sons and Lovers,* as in superficially dissimilar works like *The Rainbow, Kangaroo,* and *The Escaped Cock,* as a search for tenderness between parent and child, friends of each sex, lovers, races, man and nature, man and God. The seminal conflict in his fiction recurs between the forces of passion and intellect, as between Walter Morel and his "high-minded" wife. Indeed, the attitudes Lawrence defined in January, 1913, to assist his artist friend Ernest Collings, remained the substance of his persistent professional concern:

> My great religion is a belief in the blood, the flesh, as being wiser than the intellect. We can go wrong in our minds. But what our blood feels and believes and says is always true. The intellect is only a bit and bridle. What do I care about knowledge. All I want is to answer to my blood, direct, without fribbling intervention of mind, or moral, or what-not. I conceive a man's body as a kind of flame, like a candle flame, forever upright and yet flowing: and the intellect is just the light that is shed onto the things around. And I am not so much concerned with the things around—which is really mind—but with the mystery of the flame forever flowing, coming God knows how from out of practically nowhere, and being itself, whatever there is around it, that it lights up.

The arrogant whimsy of Lawrence's attacks on "mind" and the ethical perils of his rhapsodic "blood-percept," which Bertrand Russell (and later Ernest Seillière) pronounced the road "to Auschwitz," appear no less alarming when one recalls that Lawrence himself had been an academic, first in all England and Wales in his teachers' certifying exam, as well as a gifted mathematician. As a writer, he usually made three scrupulous drafts of each manuscript. His friend, the novelist Catherine Carswell, reports that he dismayed writers who asked his advice by accompanying refined appraisal of their work with instructions for its thorough revision. The stale heartlessness Lawrence's later novels associate with intellectuality may stem from the pragmatism he observed in the normal school and in his mother's world. There the glamour of knowledge lay not in itself but in the security and status it could provide. In any case, his ultimate celebration of the life of feeling implies a turning-away from the "sane" ambitions of Gertrude Morel. As so many critics have argued, it is perhaps no coincidence that the rhetoric of his letter's apology for the "candle flame, forever upright and yet flowing" is the same he had chosen a few months earlier to describe Walter Morel, whose sensuousness "flowed off his flesh like the flame from a candle."

II

Reviews of *Sons and Lovers* both pleased Lawrence and annoyed him. He had written Ernest Collings that he himself "admired" the book "immensely" and assured Edward Garnett that it had "form," "patiently and laboriously" constructed. On June 21, 1913, he wrote to Garnett, "I liked the reviews of *Sons and Lovers.*" Doubtless he alluded to two partially favorable reviews of the book that had appeared on that day in the London *Saturday Review* and *Athenaeum.* The *Review* applauded *Sons and Lovers* for being excelled by none of the year's important novels "in interest and power." The *Athenaeum,* whose book critic had scolded him for his *White Peacock* in 1911, objecting that the work was "needlessly frank to a fastidious mind,"[6] praised *Sons and Lovers* as a "fine . . . piece of work." But both papers rebuked Lawrence for its form. "What is wrong in the book," said the *Review's* critic,

> is the frequent intrusion of the writer. . . . Mr. Lawrence's inability to efface himself is now his most serious weakness, for the faulty construction of his earlier work is in no way evident in *Sons and Lovers.*

And the *Athenaeum* concurred:

> Mr. Lawrence's new novel is . . . not altogether a well-made piece of work. A certain distortion arises from the fact that, while all the other characters are drawn, as it were, in the third person, the hero is drawn in the first. The pronoun "I" is not, indeed, employed for him, but the author has lived so completely within his creation that the narrative reads like an autobiography—and, as discerning readers know, autobiographies are less likely than biographies to produce a lifelike portrait.

By the time Lawrence had read other cavils in the July *Standard English Review* and the more complimentary *Nation,* he grew irritated and perplexed. "Do *you* think the second half of *Sons and Lovers* such a lapse from the first," he asked Garnett, "or is it [the reviewers' objections to the 'second half'] moralistic blarney? Frieda agrees with

---

[6] The reviewer in fact affirmed that the author was a woman and spoke of him as "she."

them that Miriam and Clara and Paul's love affairs weren't worth writing about." In this case the critics seem to have anticipated the views of John Galsworthy, who would later deplore *The Rainbow*. Faithful to the traditions of the novel of manners, Galsworthy wrote Garnett in 1914 that he liked the domestic scenes in *Sons and Lovers* but not "the love part . . . It's not good enough to spend time and ink describing the penultimate sensations and physical movements of people getting into a state of rut; we all know them too well." Lawrence responded with impatience to the ambiguous consensus that *Sons and Lovers* possessed some sort of internal principle of unity but no consistent or objective point of view. "*Sons and Lovers* is supposed, technically, to have no construction," he chaffed. "The world is full of technical fools." Frieda, who felt that its flaws lay elsewhere—in failure to fulfill its own special objectives—complained to Garnett, "Why are you English so keen on [form]?" Then, years later, she wrote more confidently, "Lawrence looked at the elemental part in human beings to write about. So critics, at the time he wrote, said . . . that he had no form."

Some readers, of course, not sharing Edith Wharton's exasperation at "such a botched and bungled piece of work," welcomed *Sons and Lovers* as a great novel. Viola Meynell and Ivy Low (Litvinoff), whose own novel of adolescent "self-torment," *Growing Pains*, had been delightedly puffed in the March, 1913 *Athenaeum*, ordained that Lawrence was a genius; that those denying it "walked in darkness." Viola Meynell proceeded to offer him lodging at her home in Greatham. (The author of *Sons and Lovers* often found house-room that the writer of *The Rainbow* would have been otherwise denied.) Ivy Low acquainted him with London literati and gave him the adulation with which the Dorothy Bretts and Mabel Luhans were soon to flatter and frighten him. Among other Freudians, the psychoanalyst Dr. David Eder visited Lawrence to discuss the Oedipus complex. James M. Barrie and Amy Lowell sent letters approving *Sons and Lovers*, whose "warm, rich darkness" captivated Katherine Mansfield and John Middleton Murry. In 1914, while Lawrence busied himself with *The Rainbow*—a book, he said, "quite unlike *Sons and Lovers*, not a bit visualized"—Henry James noticed him in the *Times Literary Supplement*. There, in what the outraged Rebecca West called "scornful parenthesis," the genius who saw no genius in *Leaves of Grass* demoted the author of *Sons and Lovers* to last place in a literary steeplechase among "The Younger Generation" that included Arnold Bennett, H. G. Wells, Hugh Walpole, and Gilbert Cannon. But there was sufficient public interest in the book to earn Lawrence the nuisance of disciples and the novelty of glittering invitations to dinner. Meanwhile Lawrence's sisters in the Midlands were experiencing the effects of notoriety; for The *New York Times*' judgment that "Mr. Lawrence has small regard for conventional morality" was so richly sustained by the mining communities that Ada and Emily were mercilessly stared at out-of-doors while the memory of "mardy" ("babyish") Lawrence who "only played ring-o'-roses with young women" was loathed with relish by his father's friends. As for Lawrence, he grieved that the book, at first a *succès d'estime,* cost Duckworth 15£ in losses. By mischance, he never received a penny for the American edition, published by Kennerley and a popular success.

III

Debates about the formal merits of *Sons and Lovers* persist in our time. The most famous hypothesis of its defects is certainly Mark Schorer's discussion of "confusions between [Lawrence's] intention and performance," evident in Paul's self-centered estimates of his own and other characters' behavior, and symbolically expressed by the book's conclusion in which Paul "turns toward . . . life—as nothing in his previous history persuades us that he could unfalteringly do."[7] Describing its contradictory characterizations of Paul's parents as "a problem not only of style . . . but of point of view," Schorer reasons that "Morel and Lawrence are never separated, which is a way of saying that Lawrence maintains for himself in his book the confused attitude of his character." Louis Fraiberg decides that in *Sons and Lovers* "the author's vision exceeds his means" and agrees with Schorer that "the [discernible] split between Lawrence the man and Lawrence the writer" results in the novel's disunity and "incongruous conclusion." [8] Other critics like Horace Gregory, Dorothy Van Ghent, George H. Ford, Julian Moynihan, and Mark Spilka have parried such objections, some attempting, in Spilka's words, to trace the "strange subjective power of the novel" to structural principles dependent upon "poetic rather than narrative logic." Among others, Angus Burrell, Graham Hough, Martin Jarrett-Kerr, Harry T. Moore, Daniel A. Weiss, Mark Spilka, and Mary Freeman find no incoherence in the book's conclusion.

An effort to prove *Sons and Lovers* shapely in a "poetic" rather than a "narrative" way is doomed to failure, since those terms do not exclude each other. There is, however, a principle of unity in *Sons and Lovers:* that of antithesis, the rhythmic poise and counterpoise of polarities.

[7] Mark Schorer, "Technique as Discovery," *The Hudson Review,* I, no. 1 (Spring 1948), pp. 67–78.

[8] Louis Fraiberg, "The Unattainable Self," in *Twelve Original Essays on Great English Novels,* ed., Charles Shapiro (Detroit: Wayne State University Press, 1960), pp. 175–201.

In an unused preface to the book, exploring the anti-creative disaster of Oedipal love, Lawrence proposed that a man's work or "uttering" depends on his "com[ing] and go[ing]" to a woman not his mother: the "systole and diastole of the Heart." Three years after the completion of *Sons and Lovers,* his essay "Love" defined the vulnerable aspect of the communion Paul Morel cannot rightly achieve: "the coming together depends on the going apart; the systole depends on the diastole; the flow depends on the ebb." Finally, in "Morality and the Novel," Lawrence expressed his sense of the reciprocity and relevancy of antitheses in aesthetic terms: "life is so made that opposites sway about a trembling centre of balance. . . . And of all the art forms, the novel most of all demands the trembling and oscillating of the balance."

In *Sons and Lovers,* coherent form and responsible perspective are achieved by an earnestly balanced portrayal of contradictory impulses and points of view. Character and action are explored through paradoxes in behavior and through a series of antipodal images like space and closure, darkness and light, nature and the machine, or vitality and somnolence, by which an inclusiveness of insight is dramatized. Even as the novel rehearses contrapuntal rhythms[9] of rejection-acceptance, hate-love, or optimism-despair which it inflects over and over (as Walter Morel, for example, is seen as mean or tender, angry or piteous, crude or exquisitely polite), it locates these patterns in one consistently ambivalent psyche. Paul is, in one sense, disturbed; in another, immature; but in a third, observant—the child-father of the man who will be the narrator of *Sons and Lovers.* There is no identity between his vision and the narrator's, but rather a kind of reflexive coöperation: thus, the book's opening chapters trace the genesis of those situations and feelings that will form Paul Morel. They are spoken by a voice that has inherited its authority and knowledge from an uncertain struggle in an environment of contradictions. No other novel deals more nicely with characters who are, like Gertrude and Walter Morel, both admirably right and catastrophically wrong; or, like Miriam, wronged yet exasperating; or, like Paul, cruel—the word is used of him again and again, reminding one of Lawrence's bold dictum, "cruelty is a perverted form of sex"—yet kind. Successive scenes, "systole" and "diastole," present the victim as victimizer and the victimizer as victim while the central consciousness tries, in the phrase of *The Prelude,* to understand "the diverse shapes/That individual character presents/To an attentive eye." The narrative texture

---

[9] In his perceptive study of Lawrence's novels and stories, *Double Measure* (New York: Holt, Rinehart & Winston, Inc., 1965, p. 47), George H. Ford employs the phrases "contrasting rhythms" and "balancing one set of forces against an opposite set of forces" to interpret Lawrence's attention to paradox in a manner relative to, but different from, this essay's.

of the novel suggests not lack of focus, but the continuously faithful receptivity of an ordering consciousness in pursuit of order. As Clara and Paul, and Paul and Miriam, meet and part, the novel phrases and rephrases versions of the experience, usually deciding, not on an interpretation favorable to Paul (as Mark Schorer proposes in the case of the breach with Miriam), but on a double interpretation. And, as Schorer complains, the dual analyses which he calls "contradictions" do "appear sometimes within single paragraphs" or in a few paragraphs; but, indeed, Lawrence does not bother "to tell us which [point of view] is true"—since neither is.[10]

Thus when, after their trial "marriage" in her grandmother's cottage, Paul tells Miriam "I want us to break off," her reaction—and the motives he assigns to it—merge in uneasy dialogue: a dialogue in which key words are differently charged with all the instinctive antagonism called up at the first meeting of Paul and Miriam when the symbolic act of feeding a hen was one thing for a critical and troubled boy and another for a timid and troubled girl:

> She bent her head, pondering. He was an unreasonable child. He was like an infant which, when it has drunk its fill, throws away and smashes the cup.

> *   *   *

> "Always—it has always been so!" she cried. "It has been one long battle between us—you fighting away from me."
> He sat in silence. He was full of a feeling that she had deceived him. She had despised him when he thought she worshipped him. . . . He hated her. All these years she had treated him as if he were a hero, and thought of him secretly as an infant, a foolish child. Then why had she left the foolish child to his folly? His heart was hard against her.
> She sat full of bitterness. She had known—oh, well she had known! All the time he was away from her she had summed him up, seen his littleness, his meanness, and his folly. . . . Ah, he was not a man! He was a baby that cries for the newest toy.

Here, "right" and "wrong" are held in careful balance by the conceit, *child*. The novel's pivotal theme of bondage (see section IV, below) has one chief, though many subsidiary, emanations: that of the "navel string," the unbroken umbilicus by which Mrs. Morel feels Paul tied to her and which he tries to duplicate in binding himself to the two other women in the novel, Miriam and Clara, who suggest her spiritual and sexual aspects. The passage does not debate Miriam's acuteness in deeming Paul's behavior childish. Instead, it reveals how

[10] Cf. Graham Hough's argument that, in *Sons and Lovers,* there is no spectator character who stands apart from the action and serves as a vehicle for the novelist's point of view"; that "no [character] is right[;] no one can claim a superior insight to the others." (*The Dark Sun,* New York: The Macmillan Company, 1956, p. 51.)

differently each character interprets the dynamics of this relationship in which, with varying degrees of candor, one has agreed to play the rôle of "child" and the other that of "mother." Miriam seems partially to consent to and conserve the duplicate cord that connects Paul to her emotionally. Her lament, "it has been one long battle between us—you fighting away from me," recalls Mrs. Morel's resentful cry that Paul is growing away from her, indeed, discarding her for Miriam. But Miriam is also "normal" enough to want her lover to behave like a responsible adult: she regrets that he is "not a man"; and her words "infant" and "child" score Paul's irrational egoism. To Paul, however, they shift responsibility all the more from him to Miriam. As his pseudo-mother, certainly as the genetrix of his imaginary life, Miriam must save him from himself, even as one protects a child. He is "right" in realizing that, having rationalized into silence one whole aspect of her opinion of him, Miriam is unfair. She is "right" in deploring Paul's infantilism.

Thus by oscillating moods and *aperçus,* the novel achieves a sensitive view of a milieu in which personalities, like forces, cannot purely intermingle; whose protagonist describes his own "consciousness" as "split" and who appears to himself "one internecine battle" and economically concludes of his mother and father, "the pity was, she was too much his opposite."

If the novel's quite logical ending perplexes, relating it to the close of another confessional account of scarred but determined youth may illumine its appropriateness. Byron's world-weary aristocrat, Childe Harold, and Paul Morel, the poor man's son who joys, before his mother's death, in simplest things, are different yet alike. Both characters worry that, as Byron said of Harold, their "good and evil are at perpetual war." Paul is angry to think with "arbitrary" Miriam that he might possess rudely unreconciled "desires for higher things, and desires for lower," but this schism is attributed to him, as it is to Harold. Although Paul Morel does not share Harold's history of posturing "through sin's long labyrinth" and has hardly spent his days in "ungodly glee" among "concubines" and "flaunting wassailers," the "clear, fierce [nonconformist] morality" that makes him "anti-alcoholist," that prompts him nervously to ask Clara after adulterous lovemaking, "Not sinners, are we?" is related to the Calvinist morality that relentlessly teaches Harold his guilt. The source of guilt—heavily underlined in Byron, dramatized with terrible innocence by Lawrence —is the same: an incestuous and debilitating affection that results in Harold's "gloom" and narcissism and in Paul's hostile detachment and "sick[ness]" of heart. Indeed, a preface Byron added to his poem, republished in 1813 exactly a century before Lawrence's novel, ascribed to the poem a didactic quality that Lawrence's discarded preface also claims for *Sons and Lovers.* Childe Harold's story was to prove that "early perversion of mind and morals leads to satiety of past pleasures and disappointments in new ones . . ." Paul's story was to illustrate the emotional atrophy early accomplished by Oedipal love, that misdirected passion whose beginnings, like Paul's "hygienic" sleep against his mother's side, seem beneficial but whose end may be the denigration of personality:

> If a son-lover take a wife, then is she not his wife, she is only his bed. And his life will be torn in twain, and his wife in her despair shall hope for sons, that she may have her lover in her hour.

Byron attributes to Childe Harold an outward sign of inward sin: a "sullen," "faded," wrinkled brow which "flash[es]" with pangs of "grief . . . which he could not control." Lawrence, too, externalizes Paul's inner discord. From babyhood, all notice in him "the knitting of the . . . brows" "as if [he] were trying to understand something that was pain"; and this recurrent frown advertises the crises in Paul's anguish. Paul's difficulty, like Harold's, results in a sporadic quest for inanition, a loss of self in Nature. In his lovemaking with Miriam and Clara, Paul strives to avoid "the littleness, the personal relationship" that implicates him, even as it does Harold, in the hateful human world of "consciousness" and "responsibility." Instead, he seeks, in Byron's phrase, "to mingle with the Universe," deciding "to be alive, to be urgent and insistent—that was *not-to-be*. The highest of all was to melt out into the darkness and sway there, identified with the great Being." Yet this is not gentle communion with a refreshing Nature dramatized in the early Wordsworthian chapters of *Sons and Lovers*. In his first sexual encounter, Paul "reach[es] out to death," experiencing a kind of psychic orgasm akin to the oblivion Harold alternately craves and disdains.

The conclusive similarity between Byron's poem and Lawrence's novel is technical. To contain Harold's Manichaeism, his rhythmic ambivalence between death-wish and commitment to life in art, Byron devises the emblematic pilgrimage that moves forward in what is both escape and progress. The same rhythmic counterpoint of passions, the same thematic thrust forward and away, distinguish *Sons and Lovers*. After Mrs. Morel's death, Paul is, like Harold, devoid of ambition, sentiment, and "religion." Yet Miriam, at their final interview, observes that he moves "with a certain sureness of touch, swift and relentless and quiet." Lawrence defended Paul's decision to turn toward the town and life quite simply, saying "he had his courage left." It is a credible defense; for there is—and has always been—in Paul, as more complexly in Harold, an insistency of will, a crude responsiveness to living, that urges him on despite despair. Thus months before, though he perceived that he was "sacrificing" Miriam (like Annie's offending doll Arabella), Paul's desire for her and his

need to be a man and no longer "a youth" were able to overwhelm his
pity:

> She lay to be sacrificed for him because she loved him so much. And
> he had to sacrifice her. For a second, he wished he were sexless or dead.
> Then he shut his eyes again to her, and his blood beat back again.

Indeed, Paul's history is that of one who has learned to repel any
limiting claims. Having seduced two women, he abandons each when
he decides he has outgrown her. Loving his mother, he kills her when
her hold on life becomes painful to them both. Having already taken
such measures to survive, he would certainly persevere at the book's
close.[11]

That persistency amid ruin becomes a "voyage" of consequence is
a frequent premise of Romantic art. Childe Harold ends his travels
at Rome; but Byron's poem continues, rhapsodizing the pleasures of
"pathless woods" and praising the "freshening" vitality of Ocean on
which, it implies, the search for self may be resumed. *Sons and Lovers,*
which describes the course of Paul's pilgrimage as son, also ends with a
beginning: Paul's undertaking as man. For "derelict," the last chapter's
title, denotes first, one "left or abandoned, as by the owner or guard-
ian" (Oxford English Dictionary)—and this emphasizes the ties that
have bound Paul to mother and mistresses and that, broken, leave
his hands "inert," his body "abandoned." But a derelict is also a
wanderer. Paul, like Harold, "want[s] to rest," but he cannot "rest"
with Miriam or by his mother's grave lest he "deny . . . his own life."
It is fitting, perhaps, that a novel that alludes to Romantic and
Symbolist writers—to Wordsworth, Baudelaire, Verlaine, Poe, Scott,
and Daudet, all of whom describe journeys in search of identity—
should end with the hero's determination not to "give in"; and that
Lawrence, who claimed to have learned most from the English Ro-

[11] It is significant in this context that Part I of *Sons and Lovers* ends with the
death of Gertrude Morel's first son, William (and with the word *cemetery*) while
Part II concludes with Paul's resolve not to die (and with the word *quickly,* which
means "livingly"). Louis Fraiberg's argument that the "plan" of *Sons and Lovers*
fails because "the events do not bring associated changes in character" and because
"Paul cannot develop" as a protagonist seems, in this light, false. The arrangement
of the two parts of the novel themselves provides a tutelary contrast between the
son who has not learned to save himself and the son who has. William's sexual
generosity to an ungenerous mistress, who is no worthier of his love "than a rag
doll," far exceeds Paul's consideration of Miriam or Clara. In deciding to do the
"right thing" for Gypsy by marrying her, he fully understands that he is doing the
wrong thing for himself. His example—that of a man "who looked as if he would
go to the world's end if he wanted to" yet cannot survive his first love affair—has
obviously been a lesson to Paul. However crassly, regretfully, or precariously, Paul
manages always to break whatever ties threaten his developing need for freedom.
At the end of the book, he claims what had been William's chance: to "go abroad,"
to live differently.

mantics and who has been for fifty years compared to them, should, like Byron, conclude the chapters of his hero's defeat on a note of aspiration and modest triumph.

IV

The most inclusive theme in *Sons and Lovers* is the familiar Romantic one of bondage. Its chief expression is the "bondage" exerted upon Paul by his mother, whom he both "loves" and "hates" and from whom he earns final release by mercy-killing. The recurrence of words like "bond," "bound," "bound up," "imprisoned," "fastened," "tied up," "caught," and their cognates—"get away from" and "run away from"—establishes a rhetoric of paradox suited to this story about birth, love, and death: each is a release but also a form of capture by the forces of life and dissolution.

Sons and Lovers, although not a novel of social criticism, entertains two social problems: the effects of industrialism on human beings and the modern rôle and rights of women. Two major images, the mine and the woman, appear both as liberating and constrictive forces; in the case of woman, the force binds but is also bound. Thus, for example, the life of the mine is squalid and dangerous: it impoverishes and terrifies Morel's family and stunts his own intellect and body. On the other hand, it is a life at the earth's core, has the charm of mystery and bravery, and results in Morel's singular adaptability: he can squeeze into small places and, with a stalk from a hedge between his teeth, is "quite as happy [in the pit] as when he was in the field." Sex and alcoholism, religion and brawling, learning and social ambition, even art and nature, are all types of escape from the mine, since the people in *Sons and Lovers* are, like Paul, "prisoner[s] of industrialism." Although Minton pit lacks the paralyzing powers of Le Voreux in Zola's colliery saga, *Germinal,* with its daily "meat calls," dying horses, and moribund men, it is still, like the factory, a restrictive force. But while Le Voreux is a rapacious monster, Minton, Paul says, is "a big creature that you don't know," "beautiful" with "the feel of *men* on [it]": the source of Morel's degradation but also of his vitality.

All the characters in *Sons and Lovers* are imprisoned by their own gender. The masculine pattern of *apartheid* in the life of wakes, tavern, factory, and mine provides release from the responsibilities of work, love, and family; but it has "numbing" effects which keep men from the culminating experience of communion with women in the life process. Thus Walter Morel is "too tired" from his profitless labor at the bottom of the mine to react to Paul's birth: "what did he care about the child or [his wife]?" But Mrs. Morel, though "sick to death," rejoices, for *her* labor relates her to nature though it also commits her and her son to the allegorical equivalent of Morel's world, the Bottoms. (Paradoxically, of course, Paul's birth is the result of the "confinement" of pregnancy, that dramatic image of "bondage" with which the book opens and which translates Mrs. Morel's once light step into a heavy one and her world into a "back garden," where she feels "buried alive.")

If her femininity keeps Gertrude Morel from the vocational freedom her old beau devalues and leads to her being "tied to" Morel, womanhood impedes Miriam and Clara also. As a girl, Miriam Leivers is "not allowed to be anything," forced to clean floors instead of studying and to accept her brothers' and then Paul's "domination," which she loathes as "a sort of bondage." Clara Dawes, though "made for passion," is a suffragette with "a grudge against men." The scene between Paul, Clara, and her mother in the Radford home supports Lawrence's hypothesis that industrialism keeps woman from achieving selfhood and happiness by diverting her energies from the natural to the artificial:

> "Do you like jennying?" he asked [Clara].
> "What can a woman do!" she replied bitterly.
> "Is it sweated?"
> "More or less. Isn't *all* women's work? That's another trick the men have played, since we force ourselves into the labour market."
> "Now then, you shut up about the men," said her mother. "If the women wasn't fools, the men wouldn't be bad uns, that's what I say. No man was ever that bad wi' me but what he got it back again."

Mrs. Radford's frame of reference is not the world of business competition but of sex antagonism. Her appreciation of men originates in her having "been there," having achieved the equality through passion that Clara, as "somnambule" in marriage as is Miriam in virginity, never found with Dawes and seeks, Lawrence implies, in Woman's Rights. Clara is "denied and deprived of so much," despite that glowing physicality suggested by frequent descriptions of her "creamy arms" "full of life" next the jenny:

> [Her] arm moved mechanically, that should never have been subdued to a mechanism, and her head was bowed to the lace, that should never have been bowed. She seemed to be stranded there among the refuse that life has thrown away, doing her jennying.

Sexual love is an escape from many of the bonds the book explores; but in *Sons and Lovers,* the passion of captive men and women is unsuccessful, failing to light the "Pentecostal" "forked flame" of *Lady Chatterley's Lover.* Instead, it is another bitter if ecstatic form of bondage. Paul tells Clara that "love should give a sense of freedom, not of prison." But to him as to others, it means being "put in a pocket," "bottled up"; and Paul fears marrying Miriam because of the "physical bondage." Most marriages in the novel (and all engagements except Annie's) are missteps. Arthur, who marries his pregnant girl friend, is "caught": "it did not matter how he kicked and struggled." Pregnancy forces the factory girl Susan to marry. Mrs. Morel warns William that sex results in "a string round your neck that you can't pull off"; his death of erysipelas, a disease first visible at his neck, follows his engagement to Gypsy.

The social, psychical, and emotional bonds of love induce physical reactions—constricted breathing or desires to run or fight. Mrs. Morel "only breath[es] freely when [Morel is] gone out of the room"; Paul, faced with his desire for Miriam, has to run away "where he could breathe"; Clara, "tied for life" to Dawes, feels "fastened and bound up" and "as if [she] wanted to run." Sexuality, removed, as it is here, from the life of tenderness taught in later Lawrence novels, is no antidote to the frustrations engendered by a difficult environment and by the imperfect concord of the sexes. Yet its alternative for the adolescent Paul is virginity in which he is "bound in," "anxious and imprisoned."

Much of the radiant energy of *Sons and Lovers* rises in its consistent revelation of human quest for fulfillment despite limitation. Mrs. Morel's cornflower crockery, Paul's tube of paint, Morel's umbrella: each is a victory over the boundaries life imposes. The appetite for open space that the characters experience—Mrs. Morel's pride in "an extra strip of garden"; her flights from the tight house to the company-owned cricket field, "like the bed of a sea of light"; the children's joy in the Scargill Street "vastness"—reflects the will to survive and to transcend limits. By contrast, Paul's temptation at the end of the novel to reduce himself past even the fetal seed into the nothingness his mother's womb now represents violates the ethic of endurance that the book's imagery sustains. When he turns toward the town (and, implicitly, toward those commitments it will exact), Paul exchanges the "immense dark silence" of the bonds of death for life.

V

It is often remarked that *Sons and Lovers* employs traditional fictive techniques: colorful depiction of setting, characterization qualified by environment, and the choice of natural states to describe psychic ones (it rains, for instance, when Gertrude Morel is buried, when Miriam and Paul first make love, and when Paul leaves Clara to Dawes: rain, nature's "tears," suggesting the wretchedness generated by each of these related moments of emptiness and loss). Other traditional methods, discreetly managed, improve the story's definition and allusiveness.

Many names in *Sons and Lovers* help to explore the places and people that bear them. Thus, *Paul Morel* had used the actual name, Eastwood; but in *Sons and Lovers* Lawrence's village becomes Bestwood, an irony repeated in Paul's pathetic hypothesis that the Carrington Street canal is "just like Venice." William Morel, over-extending himself as his mother's "knight," exchanging the sordid security of the mine for London, a feckless fiancée, and dreams of Mediterranean travel, dies at a shabby flat aptly located in "Elmer's End." Just as appropriately, his fickle and wasteful "Gypsy" is not there; but the "Little Woman," as Gertrude Morel and Lydia Lawrence are both nicknamed, stands pluckily by: still, as the vernacular phrase indicates, the (surrogate) wife, related to the "Little Old Woman in the Shoe," so poor she can do little for her children but "put them to bed." Clara, both a belle and a "blue-stocking," lives on Bluebell Hill. Gertrude Morel, while she was an unmarried school teacher, fierce in her chastity and learning, lived on Minerva Terrace. Arthur Morel's turbulent and independent fiancée, whose repartee with him faintly parallels that of Shakespeare's Beatrice with Benedict, is called Beatrice Wyld.

Other names are etymologically suitable. Paul accuses Miriam of being "always sad," "bitter," and virginal. In Hebrew, "Miriam" means bitter and plaintive. It is also in Hebrew the Virgin's name. Clara from *clarus,* clear or bright, describes the effect of Clara Dawes, whose body seems so luminous to Paul that next it "all the Leivers were eclipsed like candles."

Paul, whose prophetic but separatist rôle as artist is indicated in the book, is "suddenly" given the name of his grandfather's favorite saint while Mrs. Morel offers him to the brilliant sunlight, wondering "what [he will] be." Mrs. Morel "[knows] not why" she fixes on "Paul"; but her instinct, like that of Julie in Lawrence's short story *Sun,* is undoubtedly to separate her son from his father; indeed, to relate him to her own father, a "harsh," "ironic" man "who ignored all sensuous pleasure" and "drew near in sympathy only to one man, the Apostle Paul." Her hatred of Morel, liveliest at Paul's birth, conceives this means of alienating them. (Interestingly, she wonders whether Paul will be a "Joseph" and one remembers that Joseph won his success in an alien land and in a manner different from Jacob's.) Nuances of this scene—the "crimson, throbbing" sunlight into which she thrusts the child, naming him—suggest the moment in *Acts of the Apostles,* 9:3–7, when Saul of Tarsus, blinded by a great light, becomes Paul, Apostle to the Gentiles, sent by God "into the city" where—like Paul Morel's?—his appointed tasks would be revealed. Young Paul's puritanism and poeticism do not exclude comparison with St. Paul's. Called "Postle" by other characters, he shows that intelligent, irritable dissatisfaction with things as they are, which, if directed, can lead to art or crusade.[12] It is meaningful, too, as Kingsley Widmer points out, that the child in "The Rocking-Horse Winner" is also named Paul.[13] This boy, like the small Paul Morel who picked blackberries until he was exhausted or the older Paul making Liberty prints for cash, drives himself to acquit his mother's ambition. As Widmer remarks, there is a provocative similarity between both "exceptional" sons in their efforts to prove themselves to dissatisfied mothers:

> "I never told you, mother, that if I can ride my horse, and *get there*, then I'm absolutely sure—oh, absolutely! Mother, did I ever tell you? I *am* lucky!"

> "Mother," [Paul] said, "I s'll make a painter that they'll attend to. . . . You shall see, my pigeon! You see if you're not swanky one of these days!"

To "get there" in *Sons and Lovers* is to achieve the sexual epiphany. Because of his Oedipal fascination, Paul cannot; and the rocking-horse winner's death is the result of his perverse and frustrating rôle as his mother's protector.

Inevitably, one wonders why Lawrence called Mrs. Morel "Gertrude" since his mother, whose name was Lydia (called "Little" by her son), seems to have suggested certain aspects of "Lettie" in *The White Peacock* and "Lydia" in *The Rainbow*. Obviously the erotic scene between Paul and his mother in chapter 8 bears resemblances to that between Queen Gertrude and Hamlet (and Gertrude Morel is said to have a "queenly" air) : they are interrupted by the father-husband and the scene ends with Paul, like Hamlet, begging his mother not to go to her husband's bed. Of course, in *Sons and Lovers,* the partner specifically attacked is Paul's not Gertrude's, and the incestuous climate is pronounced, not suggested.[14]

Certain episodic patterns in *Sons and Lovers,* as in many novels from Fielding to Joyce and Hemingway, seem gently to draw on legend and myth to invest Paul's story with a grander significance. So his life strikes Paul as "an Arabian nights." His first sight of Jordan's Surgical Appliances factory is accompanied with the fright, distaste, and sur-

---

[12] Lawrence himself made a crusade in print of his beliefs in sexual kindliness and had Pauline notions about the requisite dominance of husbands and the dangerousness of headstrong women. Katherine Mansfield once described him sitting in a boat at Cornwall "rather as though the people of Falmouth had cried to him as the Macedonians did to Paul and he was on his way over to help them." In his latter years, he accepted "disciples" and even wrote them moral epistles!

[13] Kingsley Widmer, *The Art of Perversity* (Seattle: University of Washington Press, 1962), p. 93.

[14] Daniel A. Weiss in his essay "The Mother in the Mind," reprinted in this volume, compares Paul to Hamlet and Miriam to Ophelia.

prise of a knight's initiation to enchantment. The boy's wretchedness in being exiled to the "business world" with its regulated system of values and its "impersonality" is matched by his artist's sense of adventure, aroused by the approach to Jordan's. Down a dark, narrow street and under "a big, dark archway," Paul and his mother venture "as into the jaws of the dragon." They go "cautiously" past a shop whose window seems threateningly animate, like a "cunning, half-shut eye." Next they reach the warehouse itself, which resembles a medieval castle and lies near Nottingham Castle. In the yard, straw "streams" "like gold" as in the fable of the malevolent child-robbing dwarf Rumpelstiltskin, though "elsewhere the place [is] like a pit." The spell cast upon Paul by Jordan's is antithetical to the "spell" Miriam's rhapsodic nature exercises, or the "spell" Mrs. Morel exerts on William by telling him stories, or the enchantment wrought upon Paul and his mother by the cathedral. It is a magic worked not by art but by need and greed. Thus the factory is "an insanitary, ancient place" through which light filters so dimly that the ground floor storehouse is a "dungeon" where workers lunch in an artificial night. Here, women are shut up in various alcoves spinning or sewing, one of them a hunchback, another like "Elaine in the *Idylls of the King*"; and their timbreless voices reach the ears of their boss, or jailer, through a tube.

Traditional fables about spinners and weavers blend in Paul's imagination. He compares Clara to Penelope waiting for Ulysses: "there is always about [her] . . . a sort of waiting." The girls' spinning is a postponement of life. Clara, "somnambule," is a type of Sleeping Beauty who "went to sleep as [she] grew to be a woman," altered not by the life-giving phallus but by industrialism's spinning needle. Interviewing the boy Paul, elfin Mr. Jordan looks unprepossessingly like "a Pomeranian dog"; but he is master and so able to lock Paul's tongue and wits and "ma[ke] . . . a clod of him." Lawrence spent only three months in a factory; but Paul stays thirteen years, during which time he learns how to draw and how to love and work more and more mechanically. Committed by his mother to the dark recesses of the warehouse as to the womb, he does not use his own magic, art, to escape. Instead, the company, which makes wooden legs for amputees, names him overseer and by the book's end, Paul is himself an emotional amputee.

Important experiences with Miriam and Clara have fantastic and symbolic undercurrents. With Miriam, Paul explores Wingfield Manor, where Mary Queen of Scots may have been imprisoned for being, as Paul puts it, "lively." The manor, a partial ruin, has winding staircases and a tower with a broken top. Paul escorts Miriam "in the purest manner of chivalry." But later in the novel, before his "test" and "defeat" of her, Miriam, feeling she is to be "sacrificed," puts on a blouse that reminds her of Queen Mary. The irony is didactic. The flawed female-male symbols, staircase and tower, and the choice of a queen punished for illicit eroticism imply the disaster that awaits Miriam if she sleeps with Paul: she will, at the novel's close, "feel . . . dead," even as she imagined Mary feeling at Wingfield.[15]

When Paul visits Clara for the first time, he goes at night, that half of his day and life to be appointed her. She lives with a watchful mother on "a mean little street" in an old house and wears ugly clothes, her circumstances concealing her beauty as, in so many Cinderella tales and fables of metamorphosis, the surroundings hide the heroine.

Still more associations have faintly mythic qualities. George H. Ford has written of the Pluto-Persephone myth which he discerns in Law-

---

[15] One of the qualities of *Sons and Lovers* is the resonance of these symbolic episodes, their symbolic content struck out with what seems an ease and instinctiveness yielded at some moment where life and art meet to transcend each other's margins. For instance, in chapter 8 ("Strife in Love") which treats Paul's "battle" between his mother and Miriam, the first of a few attacks of weakness experienced by Mrs. Morel occurs after Paul burns the bread she has put in the oven and asked him to watch. Paul has been entertaining not only Miriam but also Arthur's girl, Beatrice, who flirts with and kisses him. Just as he offers to kiss her back, Miriam smells Mrs. Morel's bread burning. Beatrice, assuming the pose Paul's mother and sister soon adopt, blames Miriam, saying rather cruelly (since it has been she, not Miriam, who rouses Paul sexually and distracts him from the bread), "This is what comes of the oblivion of love, my boy." Paul, feeling "guilty" toward his mother *and* Miriam, walks Miriam home and returns to find the "offending" burnt loaf on the kitchen table and his mother sitting "white as a sheet" and "bluish round the mouth" in the rocker where she once nursed him, complaining that her heart hurts. Directly afterward, Paul agrees to give up Miriam and he and Mrs. Morel exchange the passionate kiss that Paul will later repeat—on the mouth—when she is dead. The psychology of the episode is immediately intelligible; it is an early analogue to the one in chapter 13 in which his mother becomes bedridden while he is on vacation. However, the incident provides another provocative instance of that radical yet subtle symbolic justice typical of *Sons and Lovers* (and so seductive to "Freudian" interpretation). In discussing "Symbolism in Dreams" in the lectures that form his *General Introduction to Psychoanalysis,* Freud ordains that "an oven stands for a woman or the mother's womb" and quotes Herodotus to suggest that putting bread into an oven is a metaphor of sexual intercourse. (Indeed, in the vulgar of many languages including English, to say that "the bread is in the oven" is to say that a woman is pregnant.) Mrs. Morel and Paul usually share the Friday night baking: it is he who makes and inserts the last, burnt loaves. As is evident from her reaction to his forgetfulness, she regards his watching the bread "grow" in the oven as a trust. Throughout the scene with Miriam and Beatrice, the process whereby the bread—a "new" thing mother and son make together—is finished, then ruined, signals the stages in Paul's sexual dalliance (and, hence, unfaithfulness to his mother). He offers to pay for the bread; but the loaf, described as "unswathed" on the table, like a new-born but "desiccated" child, can be atoned for only by his promise to continue the pseudo-sexual relationship with his mother which the baking process—like the motif of the house they will someday share—suggests. Of course, one could go on interminably in this vein, since Freud is very generous with a series of symbols—flowers as representative of "female sexual organs," gardens as symbolic of "the female genitalia," the acts of climbing towers, staircases, and hills as symbols of sexual intercourse—which Lawrence seems naturally to use.

rence's treatment of Gertrude and Walter Morel.[16] The choice Paul is forced to make among his mother, Miriam, and Clara—Miriam who is called a disguised "princess" (like Jessie Chambers, whom Lawrence called "Princess"), Clara the "Queen of Sheba," and Gertrude "Queen Victoria"—also touches on myth. When Paris chooses Aphrodite or passion above the cerebral love of Athene and the protection of Hera, mother of gods, he is rewarded with a similar "baptism of fire" in love which results, as it does for Paul, in destruction. Clara, a kind of Venus, is, like her, married to a smith whom she cuckolds. Miriam, emphatically virginal and described as having "a bloodhound quality," suggests Artemis, the chaste huntress goddess of the hounds, who—like the unwitting Miriam—often repaid her lovers with psychic or actual death.

All these associations enlarge the scope of *Sons and Lovers,* lending it mythic resonance and auguring the continuum of the marvelous in the actual and the participation of the literary and legendary in the real, especially for young men and artists.

VI

Most critics consider *The Rainbow* and *Women in Love* D. H. Lawrence's best fiction. *Sons and Lovers* is often assessed as a preliminary exercise in or quest for the Lawrentian form, a median work between what Lawrence himself called the "ordinary," "dull, old, dead" novel of "character" and "moral scheme" and the "new" novel that revealed "allotropic states": the "carbon" of human nature as opposed to its history as a "diamond." Nevertheless, although Lawrence himself had greater respect for his later novels, the ordinary reader prefers *Sons and Lovers.* Why?

There is, of course, the fascination with the biographical, always aroused by Lawrence's writing and most of all by this account of his growing-up. Like *Du Côté de chez Swann,* which appeared in the same year, *Sons and Lovers* implies an unusually rapt relationship between life and art that affirms the dimension of each and grants purpose to both. Many readers enjoy feeling beyond or behind the imaginary world of this novel the life experience that has been reconstructed and recaptured there: made to "happen again" but given, as in our own reveries about our own pasts, a demonstrable meaning. The story itself, like Joyce's *Portrait of the Artist,* published three years later, traces a process of growth, alienation, and discovery that typifies most men's development; and it concerns itself with what Emily Dickinson called the only things that matter—love and death. It satisfies the basic

---

[16] See his essay reprinted in this volume, pp. 64–73.

hunger that is also catered to by the shifting array of transient best-
sellers: the need to observe freshly and try to understand the mysteries
of innocence and knowledge, self and the family, sexuality and intellect, being and dying. Because the technique used in *Sons and Lovers*
is, as Lawrence called it, "that hard, violent style full of sensation and
presentation," it is comfortingly accessible; it also escapes the mo-
notony, abstraction, and polemics into which Lawrence's efforts to
disclose the inner self sometimes force his later prose.

Lawrence himself recognized a thematic universality in *Sons and
Lovers*: "It is a great tragedy," he told Garnett, "the tragedy of
thousands of young men in England." What Frank O'Connor terms
"the dilemma of a sensitive boy between the conflicting claims of
mother and sweetheart" may, indeed, be "an element that could only
have come from the New Men [created by the Education Act of 1870]
and the industrial areas"; and in this respect, *Sons and Lovers* has
historical, psychological, sociological, and regional significance. But the
primary triangle it depicts—not that of son, mother, and sweetheart
but of father, mother, and child—is one which empowers the oldest
myths as well as their newest equivalents and is of universal perti-
nence. That he had written *Sons and Lovers* seemed an irrelevant fact
to the later Lawrence; to many of his readers it remains the supreme
proof of his gifts as a novelist.

The essays in this volume have been chosen for their individual
merits and also to indicate the variety of critical inference drawn from
Sons and Lovers. Virginia Woolf's "Notes on D. H. Lawrence" contains factual errors and, with its concentration on what it considers
Lawrence's concentration on the "moment," it shows the tendency
of many masterly writers to find their own ideas in the books of
others. Nonetheless it is an interesting impression of *Sons and Lovers*
by one of Lawrence's distinguished if unsympathetic contemporaries.
In "The Mother in the Mind," Daniel A. Weiss discusses the effects
of Paul's Oedipal fascination and argues that in "choosing the town,
Paul is accepting his father . . . [and] rejecting, or at least modifying,
his acceptance of the mother." Keith Sagar's essay on *Sons and Lovers*
considers the "[relative] rightness" of Gertrude Morel and decides that
Paul turns to the town "to voice his mother's values against his own
temptation" to follow her in death. In "Counterfeit Loves," Mark
Spilka interprets the novel as "the successful dramatization of three
destructive forms of love—oedipal, spiritual, and 'unbalanced—possessive.'" George H. Ford's "The 'S' Curve: Persephone to Pluto" analyzes the story of the Morels as "a variant of the classical myth of
Persephone." "Sons, Lovers and Mothers" by Alfred Kazin suavely
views the novel as a revelation of the quintessential Lawrence, man
and writer.

Note on the Appendix to this Edition

May Chambers Holbrook's memoirs of D. H. Lawrence as a boy and of the Lawrence family are not, of course, literary criticism. But they provide a vivid account of the situations Lawrence translated into fiction: the courtship and death of his brother Ernest (William Morel); his mother's hatred of his father, jealousy of her sons, and concern about money; "Bert" 's (Paul Morel's) affection for flowers, books, and the Haggs farm, and his anxiety about his parents. Told by a playmate who was nevertheless an "outsider" to that explosive family group, these memoirs, with their cool view of Lydia Lawrence and their frank awareness of "Bert" 's problems and differences, provide a perspective for viewing the novel itself as a separate, selective entity ultimately independent of the experiences that engendered it.

Notes on D. H. Lawrence

by Virginia Woolf

The partiality, the inevitable imperfection of contemporary criticism can best be guarded against, perhaps, by making in the first place a full confession of one's disabilities, so far as it is possible to distinguish them. Thus by way of preface to the following remarks upon D. H. Lawrence, the present writer has to state that until April 1931 he was known to her almost solely by reputation and scarcely at all by experience. His reputation, which was that of a prophet, the exponent of some mystical theory of sex, the devotee of cryptic terms, the inventor of a new terminology which made free use of such words as solar plexus and the like, was not attractive; to follow submissively in his tracks seemed an unthinkable aberration; and as chance would have it, the few pieces of his writing that issued from behind this dark cloud of reputation seemed unable to rouse any sharp curiosity or to dispel the lurid phantom. There was, to begin with, *Trespassers,* a hot, scented, overwrought piece of work, as it seemed; then *A Prussian Officer,* of which no clear impression remained except of starting muscles and forced obscenity; then *The Lost Girl,* a compact and seamanlike piece of work, stuffed with careful observation rather in the Bennett manner; then one or two sketches of Italian travel of great beauty, but fragmentary and broken off; and then two little books of poems, *Nettles and Pansies,* which read like the sayings that small boys scribble upon stiles to make housemaids jump and titter.

Meanwhile, the chants of the worshippers at the shrine of Lawrence became more rapt; their incense thicker and their gyrations more mazy and more mystic. His death last year gave them still greater liberty and still greater impetus; his death, too, irritated the respectable; and it was the irritation roused by the devout and the shocked, and the ceremonies of the devout and the scandal of the shocked,

"Notes on D. H. Lawrence." From The Moment and Other Essays, *by Virginia Woolf (New York: Harcourt, Brace & World, Inc.; London: Hogarth Press, Ltd., 1948), pp. 93–98. Copyright 1948 by Harcourt, Brace & World Inc. Reprinted by permission of Quentin Bell, Angelica Garnett, and the publishers.*

The Mother in the Mind

by Daniel A. Weiss

Gertrude Morel moves through *Sons and Lovers* like a cry of pain. Her truth is valid only as she is an expression of her son's anguish—and this both in spite of and because of the clinical verisimilitude with which Lawrence images her as the Jocasta par excellence. Of the other characters it can be said that Lawrence is truly their creator, since they live in obedience to their own laws. But of Gertrude Morel he is merely the undertaker, responsible for her careful embalming. Her likeness is a magnificent death mask. Around her cluster the metaphors of queenliness, and virginity, and youth, the mechanically collated evidence of the Oedipal relationship. Her son William was like her knight who wore *her* favor in the battle." When she goes into town with Paul, they feel "the excitement of lovers having an adventure together." "She was gay like a sweetheart. . . . As he saw her hands in their old black gloves getting the silver out of the worn purse, his heart contracted with pain of love for her."
The inevitable wish of the child that his mother remain young becomes the conscious theme of Paul's outbursts:

"Why can't a man have a *young* mother? What is she old for? . . . And why wasn't I the oldest son? Look—they say the young ones have the advantage—but look, *they* had the young mother. You should have had me for your eldest son."
"I didn't arrange it," she remonstrated. "Come to consider you're as much to blame as me." He turned on her, white, his eyes furious.

Here the subtle disguise Paul's wish wears is the important thing. His real desire is to be even more than the "oldest son," is not even that his mother remain young, but that they be equal in age no matter what it is.
Lawrence completely idealizes Gertrude's maternal role as the mother of the infant Paul. She is Rachel, the virginal mother.

Mrs. Morel watched the sun sink from the glistening sky, leaving a soft, flower-blue overhead. . . . A few shocks of corn in a corner of the fallow

that drove one at last to read *Sons and Lovers* in order to see whether, as so often happens, the master is not altogether different from the travesty presented by his disciples.
This then was the angle of approach, and it will be seen that it is an angle that shuts off many views and distorts others. But read from this angle, *Sons and Lovers* emerged with astonishing vividness, like an island from off which the mist has suddenly lifted. Here it lay, clean cut, decisive, masterly, hard as rock, shaped, proportioned by a man who, whatever else he might be—prophet or villain, was undoubtedly the son of a miner who had been born and bred in Nottingham. But this hardness, this clarity, this admirable economy and sharpness of the stroke are not rare qualities in an age of highly efficient novelists. The lucidity, the ease, the power of the writer to indicate with one stroke and then to refrain indicated a mind of great power and penetration. But these impressions, after they had built up the lives of the Morels, their kitchens, food, sinks, manner of speech, were succeeded by another far rarer, and of far greater interest. For after we have exclaimed that this coloured and stereoscopic representation of life is so like that surely it must be alive—like the bird that pecked the cherry in the picture—one feels, from some indescribable brilliance, sombreness, significance, that the room is put into order. Some hand has been at work before we entered. Casual and natural as the arrangement seems, as if we had opened the door and come in by chance, some hand, some eye of astonishing penetration and force, has swiftly arranged the whole scene, so that we feel that it is more exciting, more moving, in some ways fuller of life than one had thought real life could be, as if a painter had brought out the leaf or the tulip or the jar by pulling a green curtain behind it. But what is the green curtain that Lawrence has pulled so as to accentuate the colours? One never catches Lawrence—this is one of his most remarkable qualities —"arranging." Words, scenes flow as fast and direct as if he merely traced them with a free rapid hand on sheet after sheet. Not a sentence seems thought about twice; not a word added for its effect on the architecture of the phrase. There is no arrangement that makes us say: "Look at this. This scene, this dialogue has the meaning of the book hidden in it." One of the curious qualities of *Sons and Lovers* is that one feels an unrest, a little quiver and shimmer in his page, as if it were composed of separate gleaming objects, by no means content to stand still and be looked at. There is a scene of course; a character; yes, and people related to each other by a net of sensations; but these are not there—as in Proust—for themselves. They do not admit of prolonged exploraton, of rapture in them for the sake of rapture, as one may sit in front of the famous hawthorn hedge in *Swann's Way* and look at it. No, there is always something further on, another goal. The impatience, the need for getting on beyond the ob-

ject before us, seem to contract, to shrivel up, to curtail scenes to their barest, to flash character simply and starkly in front of us. We must not look for more than a second; we must hurry on. But to what?

Probably to some scene which has very little to do with character, with story, with any of the usual resting places, eminences, and consummations of the usual novel. The only thing that we are given to rest upon, to expand upon, to feel to the limits of our powers is some rapture of physical being. Such for instance is the scene when Paul and Miriam swing in the barn. Their bodies become incandescent, glowing, significant, as in other books a passage of emotion burns in that way. For the writer it seems the scene is possessed of a transcendental significance. Not in talk nor in story nor in death nor in love, but here as the body of the boy swings in the barn.

But, perhaps, because such a state cannot satisfy for long, perhaps because Lawrence lacks the final power which makes things entire in themselves, the effect of the book is that stability is never reached. The world of *Sons and Lovers* is perpetually in process of cohesion and dissolution. The magnet that tries to draw together the different particles of which the beautiful and vigorous world of Nottingham is made is this incandescent body, this beauty glowing in the flesh, this intense and burning light. Hence whatever we are shown seems to have a moment of its own. Nothing rests secure to be looked at. All is being sucked away by some dissatisfaction, some superior beauty, or desire, or possibility. The book therefore excites, irritates, moves, changes, seems full of stir and unrest and desire for something withheld, like the body of the hero. The whole world—it is a proof of the writer's remarkable strength—is broken and tossed by the magnet of the young man who cannot bring the separate parts into a unity which will satisfy him.

This allows, partly at least, of a simple explanation. Paul Morel, like Lawrence himself, is the son of a miner. He is dissatisfied with his conditions. One of his first actions on selling a picture is to buy an evening suit. He is not a member, like Proust, of a settled and satisfied society. He is anxious to leave his own class and to enter another. He believes that the middle class possess what he does not possess. His natural honesty is too great to be satisfied with his mother's argument that the common people are better than the middle class because they possess more life. The middle class, Lawrence feels, possess ideas; or something else that he wishes himself to have.[1] This is one cause of his unrest. And it is of profound importance. For the

[1] [Actually, it is not Mrs. Morel but Paul who claims in chapter 10 to draw "life itself, warmth" from "the common people." She replies that although he says he dislikes ideas which come from "the middle classes," his only associates are those who exchange ideas; and she accuses him of an inverse "snobbish(ness)" about class built on illusions about the common man.]

fact that he, like Paul, was a miner's son, and that he dislik ditions, gave him a different approach to writing from have a settled station and enjoy circumstances which allo forget what those circumstances are.

Lawrence received a violent impetus from his birth. It s at an angle from which it took some of its most marked chai He never looked back at the past, or at things as if they were of human psychology, nor was he interested in literature as Everything has a use, a meaning, is not an end in itself. C him again with Proust, one feels that he echoes nobody, con tradition, is unaware of the past, of the present save as it future. As a writer, this lack of tradition affects him immer thought plumps directly into his mind; up spurt the ser round, as hard, as direct as water thrown out in all directio impact of a stone. One feels that not a single word has been c its beauty, or for its effect upon the architecture of the sente

stood up as if alive; she imagined them bowing; perhaps her son would be a Joseph. . . .

Gertrude's virginal quality expresses itself chiefly in floral arrangements. She soothes herself with "the scent of flowers"; she is Flora, never Ceres, having long ago chosen between her son's moss rose and Walter Morel's unhappy, hairy coconut.

The necessity for this purity rests, not with Gertrude, but with Paul. It is his wish that she remain pure. Freud suggests that "the grown man's conscious mind likes to regard the mother as the personification of impeccable moral purity" out of an unconscious jealousy of the father and a horror of adult sexuality. And E. T., writing of Lawrence's disgust at hearing "commercial travellers" talking on a train, remembers "that the whole question of sex had for him the fascination of horror, and also that in his repudiation of any possibility of a sex relation between us he felt that he paid me a deep and subtle compliment." The nature of the compliment will be taken up in connection with a discussion of Miriam.

Yet through the mask of Lawrence's mother there emerge occasionally the living signs of the deathly relationship between Paul and Gertrude Morel. Gertrude's careful distinction between the mind and the body, made originally in her relations with William when she refuses to acknowledge his manhood and its needs, leads, in her life with Paul, to a love affair of the spirit. And with Paul she is freer to lead it, for it is with his complicity. When Paul's picture wins a prize at the Castle, Mrs. Morel cries, "Hurrah my boy! I knew we should do it!" as if it were a child they had borne between them.

Confronted with Paul's mistresses she directs most of her bitterness against the one who most resembles herself, Miriam, the one whom Paul likewise recognizes as his mother's rival. Her judgments of Miriam are true for both of them: " 'She is one of those who will want to suck a man's soul out till he has none of his own left,' she said to herself; 'and he is just such a baby as to let himself be absorbed. She will never let him become a man; she never will.' " . . .

. . . When we consider Clara Dawes we find Lawrence attributing to Gertrude a preference for her rather than for Miriam. It is the expression of a wish whose fulfillment would preserve the spiritual nexus in which Paul and Gertrude meet as lovers. The addition of Clara (who, as we shall see, did not exist but had to be invented) to the relationship would provide a *modus vivendi* for both mother and son. Gertrude is made to see this:

> Mrs. Morel considered. She would have been glad now for her son to fall in love with some woman who would—she did not know what. But he fretted so, got so furious suddenly, and again was melancholic. She wished he knew some nice woman—She did not know what she wished, but left it vague.

For Clara represents the dancing side of the relationship, which neither she nor Miriam could provide. And both Gertrude and Miriam give Clara to him in order to purge his spiritual nature of its fleshly dress and to have him back refined and virginal. But it is important to remember that it is Paul who is the unconscious seeker, and the one, ultimately, who realizes the need Clara can satisfy in him. Mrs. Morel's compliance with the idea of Clara is the compliance of a woman putting her child out to wet-nurse. For Paul the sexuality Clara offers is feasible incest, just as his relationship with Miriam, although consummated, is not; and both relationships are determined by the root of Oedipal relationship.

The death of Lawrence's mother came about as the result of natural causes; the death of Mrs. Morel has the tragic inevitability of Clytemnestra's murder or Jocasta's suicide. It is the sequel to revelation, which presents two equally horrid alternatives to the protagonist: either the conscious continuation of an unnatural relationship, or the cessation by death of any such possibility. I have suggested that the artist of *Sons and Lovers* brought the passional side of his affair with his mother to a halt when it threatened to become an enormity. Symptomatic of that enormity were the recognition by the father of the "mischief" Paul and his mother were up to and the subsequent beginnings of a real physical struggle between father and son. It is the mother's fainting, not her death but the simulacral prefiguring of her death, that brings about Paul's search in the ensuing chapters of the novel for a mother substitute, if not a way out completely. The enfeebling of Gertrude puts her beyond being desirable as a sexual object, the girl who could race up a hill and who attracted Walter Morel. More and more, fuller and deeper complexities of "terror, agony, and love" are injected into the descriptions of Paul's love for his mother: "His life wanted to free itself of her. It was like a circle where life turned back on itself, and got no further." It is at this point that he is sexually involved, for the first time with some success, with Clara, the younger rival in a new triangle. His open, terrible, revealing fight with Baxter Dawes is followed, as his narrowly avoided fight with Walter Morel is followed, by another failure in Gertrude's health, this time a fatal one.

The recognition, as Lawrence consciously indicates it, is now complete. And his task, as before, is to render its consummation impossible. Now, in accord with the old myth, following the parricide and the achieved marriage (with both Clara and Miriam), the mother must be destroyed. "He and his mother seemed almost to avoid each other. There was some secret between them which they could not bear. He was not aware of it. He only knew that his life seemed unbalanced, as if it were going to smash into pieces." Gertrude's cancer comes as a relief to this stalemate, like the diabolical fulfillment of an oracle.

For at the heart of Paul's anguish lies an unconscious awareness of the secondary advantage to be gained from her death—she will be preserved to him. One of his great wishes has been that she remain young and uncorrupted, virginal. As the terminator of life, death is also the preserver of life, a bitter truism that suicides must intuitively grasp, pinching their lives off to anticipate destruction. Gertrude, dying, gathers to herself the imagery of youth:

> He sat down by the bed, miserably. She had a way of curling and lying on her side, like a child. The grey and brown hair was loose over her ear.
> "Doesn't it tickle you?" he said, gently putting it back.
> "It does," she replied.
> His face was near hers. Her blue eyes smiled straight into his, like a girl's—warm, laughing with tender love. It made him pant with terror, agony, and love.

And with her death the transformation is complete. She becomes the fulfillment of his wish: "She lay like a maiden asleep. With his candle in his hand, he bent over her. She lay like a girl asleep and dreaming of her love. . . . She was young again. . . . She would wake up. She would lift her eyelids. She was with him still." . . .

Gertrude's death gives rise in Paul to a very dangerous line of thought: that in dying he will be with his mother; just as the minister promises Gertrude that she will be with her son William. "Sometimes they looked into each other's eyes. Then they almost seemed to make an agreement. It was almost as if he were agreeing to die also." Paul waters her milk to weaken her, and finally he administers an overdose of morphia to her—all as if he were sending her ahead to an assignation.

> "What are you doing?" said Annie.
> "I s'll put 'em in her night milk."
> Then they both laughed together like two conspiring children. On top of all their horror flickered this little sanity.

What gives the death of Gertrude its special intensity and importance—Paul's reaction to it is the point on which the novel resolves itself—is the unwritten confusion in the artist's mind. Gertrude's death is at once a real death and a sexual death. Never is she described with such amorous concern as when she is on her deathbed, dreaming her young dream. She is, for the first time in the novel, sexually desirable and seemingly available to the son. His only rival skulks below stairs and will not even look at her. Walter Morel is afraid of her. Only Paul is her lover. "They all stood back. He kneeled down and put his face to hers and his arms round her: 'My love—my love—oh, my love!' he whispered again and again. 'My love—oh, my love.'"
But the agent that brings about both these deaths, Death itself, is Fate, God, the father in his destructive phase. Paul's speeding of Gertrude's

death is simply one more attempt to interpose himself between his father and his mother. Even when she first becomes sick, his attempt to save her is halfhearted. He knows she must die.

And finally, when he kisses her "passionately" and feels a "coldness against his mouth," he is brought to a last realization and choice. Like Baxter with Clara, he cannot get "at her." He must, as he does with Baxter Dawes, return her to the father, or else, in a continuation to the end of the closed circle, follow his mother into death for the sake of her embrace. William, Paul's brother, of whom he was "unconsciously jealous," faced the same choice earlier in the novel. Preoccupied, like Paul, with death, he anticipates his mother and prepares a place in the grave before her. Like Gertrude's death, William's death *really* happened to Lawrence's brother Ernest; what is more important, as in Gertrude's death, is that William's death *must* happen in *Sons and Lovers* to justify William's part in the novel. William's is the way not taken, the negation of Paul's choice. William's way is consciously rejected, at the end of the novel, by Paul: " 'Mater, my dear—' he began, with the whole force of his soul. Then he stopped. He would not say it. He would not admit that he wanted to die, to have done. He would not own that life had beaten him, or that death had beaten him."

Freud postulates the unconscious "conditions of love" that govern the objects of the affections of certain men. The more urgent of these conditions Freud terms "the need for an injured third party," that is, the Oedipal man's choice of woman will require that she be attached to someone else, lover or husband, who has some "right of possession" over her. The second condition, operating as a corollary to the first, requires that the woman be in some way "sexually discredited," the subject of gossip, "loose," or openly promiscuous. With the fulfillment of these conditions the lover conceives of his role as being that of rescuer, rescuing the woman he loves from moral, economic, or social ruin.

The etiology of these strange patterns of choice and response, says Freud, is identical with the normal pattern of love:

> They are derived from the infantile fixation of tender feelings on the mother, and represent one of the consequences of that fixation. In normal love, only a few characteristics survive, which reveal unmistakably the maternal prototype of the object-choice; as, for instance, the preference shown by young men for mature women; the detachment of libido from the mother has been effected relatively swiftly. In our type, on the other hand, the libido has remained attached to the mother for so long, even after the onset of puberty, that the maternal characteristics remain in the love-objects that are chosen later, and all these turn into easily recognizable mother-surrogates.

The "injured third party" is immediately recognizable as the father, in the family situation as the child first conceives of it, with the mother as the sole object of his love. The choice of the "loose" woman seems at first paradoxical, since men tend normally to think of their mothers as being morally impeccable. But the preference derives from the unstable amalgam the son must construct from things as he wants them and things as they are. His first response, upon learning about adult sexuality, is to deny his mother's complicity in such an act. And then, when he can no longer cling to the logical absurdity of such a denial, he swings with a "cynical logic" to the identification of his mother with any sexually available woman:

> The enlightening information he has received has in fact awakened the memory-traces of the impressions and wishes of his early infancy, and these have led to a reactivation in him of certain mental impulses. He begins to desire the mother herself in the sense with which he has recently become acquainted, and to hate his father anew as a rival who stands in the way of his wish; he comes, as we say, under the dominance of the Oedipus complex. He does not forgive his mother for having granted the favors of sexual intercourse not to himself but to his father, and he regards it as an act of unfaithfulness. . . . As a result of the constant, combined operation of the two driving forces, desire and thirst for revenge, phantasies of the mother's unfaithfulness are by far the most preferred; the lover with whom she commits her act of infidelity almost always exhibits the features of the boy's own ego, or more accurately, of his own idealized personality, grown up and so raised to a level with his father.

Ernest Jones refers to a similar deviation in object choice when he discusses Hamlet's sexual revulsion, his cruel abuse of Ophelia, and his "complex reaction" toward his mother:

> The underlying theme relates ultimately to the splitting of the mother image which the infantile consciousness effects into two opposite pictures: one of the virginal madonna, an inaccessible saint towards whom all sensual approaches are unthinkable, and the other of a sensual creature accessible to everyone. . . .
> When sexual repression is highly pronounced, as with Hamlet, then both types of women are found to be hostile: the pure one out of resentment at her repulses, the sensual one out of the temptation she offers to plunge into guiltiness. Misogyny, as in the play, is the result.

Miriam's contribution to the composite mother image is her purity. She is the "virginal madonna," the "virtuous and reputable woman," the "personification of impeccable moral purity," that aspect of the mother image that represents the spiritual, the physically untouchable. . . .

Upon Miriam, Lawrence heaps even more extravagant attributes of purity than upon Gertrude Morel, who has in some degree "fallen" through her marriage a victim to sexuality. Miriam is a *religieuse*. . . . Her resemblance to Ophelia approaches paraphrase. Paul writes to

Miriam *after* the turning point that follows his passionate avowal to
his mother and fight with his father: " '. . . You see I can give you a
spirit love, I have given it you this long, long time; but not embodied
passion. See, you are a nun. I have given you what I would give a holy
nun—as a mystic monk to a holy nun.' " Again this is a symbol based
on actuality. E. T. records a letter Lawrence sent her: " 'Look, you
are an nun. I give you what I would give a holy nun. You must let me
marry a woman I can kiss and embrace and make the mother of my
children.' "

Having raised Miriam to the status of the virgin mother, Paul,
because of his sexual repression, is full of "resentment at her re-
pulses." . . . The juxtaposition here of a consciously made choice of
a loved object, Paul's mother, with whom only an attenuated spiritual
communion would be possible, and a resolution to do "battle" with
another loved object, with whom more than this communion would
eventually be possible, suggests an identification of the two. In Paul's
mind Miriam has become too firmly established as a mother surrogate.
He must shake her loose. His final desperate suggestion to her that
they become lovers represents the attempt to dislodge his mother from
Miriam, the young girl, "full-breasted and luxuriantly formed." But
even this wish, when it is granted, fails, and Paul remains, with her,
Oedipus, doomed perpetually to stand on the steps of the palace and
abide his incest.

From the very beginning Lawrence assigns to Miriam the maternal
attributes that so embittered the real woman behind her. . . .

. . . It is Miriam's refusal to allow [Paul] to regress to the Nirvana,
the paradisal state of the infant, her insistence that he recognize her,
that fills him with anguish. His further accusation of Miriam clarifies
this. Paul makes his plea for the impersonality of passion, which Miriam denies him:

> . . . she wanted him to look at her with eyes full of love. His eyes full
> of the dark impersonal fire of desire, did not belong to her.
> "To be rid of our individuality, which is our will, which is our effort—
> to live effortless, a kind of conscious sleep—that is very beautiful, I think;
> that is our afterlife—our immortality." [he said]

Here in these few sentences is an adumbration of that "drift toward
death" as Lawrence sublimated it into the passional relationship par
excellence between men and women. But implicit in it here is the ultimate regression to the child's status with its mother. In his final
achievement of a sexual union between them, Paul, more strongly
than ever, identifies Miriam with his mother—but not his mother alive,
in spite of the fact that her death is still remote; that identification
would be too painful. Just as his mother's lips were cold to his passionate kiss, he realizes, after his orgasm, that Miriam "had not been with

him all the time, that her soul had stood apart in a sort of horror."
But still with this virginal woman there is a pleasure:

> . . . To him now, life seemed a shadow, day a white shadow; night, and
> day, and stillness and inaction, this seemed like *being*. To be alive to be
> urgent and insistent—that was *not-to-be*. The highest of all was to melt
> out into the darkness and sway there, identified with the great Being.

The pleasure is deadly: the road to Thebes again, which for a moment he agrees to take, and which, in the end, he will not take. In the
end the same wish is distasteful to him, and described in a tone of
horror, after his mother's death: ". . . the tear in the veil, through
which his life seemed to drift slowly, as if he were drawn toward death.
He wanted someone of their own free initiative to help him." But in
his first intercourse with Miriam he seems to be insisting that she be a
mother before she has a name. . . .

Paul misses in Miriam-as-mother the presence of the "injured third
party" and tries, as he tried to shift his own emotional passivity, to
thrust Miriam into the maternal situation. His attempts follow, as we
can almost predict they will follow, the "recognition" scene with his
parents. The offering of the role is disguised as a tender concern, the
wish that Miriam would become interested in someone else, for fear
her family would insist upon a formal engagement. "Do you think—
if I didn't come up so much—you might get to like somebody else—
another man?" The attempts fail, and with the failure the relationship,
in Freudian terms, loses one of its most important underpinnings.

While Miriam cannot produce an "injured third party" to satisfy
Paul's unconscious need for a rival, she is capable of fulfilling the
mother-love role in another way, which is an even more striking insight
into the true nature of Paul's relationships with all three women.
Throughout *Sons and Lovers* we notice a chiasmus of "giving," on the
parts of the women, with varying shades of approval and disapproval.
The first woman to give is of course Gertrude. She "gives" William's
girls to Walter Morel by purposely confusing the father and son. In the
repressed phantasy of the son the act appears to be a diverting of the
father that leaves the mother free for the son. Later, with great reluctance she gives William up to the girl he is engaged to. But the results
are fatal.

Miriam's act of giving coincides exactly with Gertrude Morel's approval of Clara for Paul, as something he needs, as something neither
of them can give him. Gertrude, considering Clara, refuses to define
her approval: "She did not know what she wished, but left it vague.
At any rate she was not hostile to the idea of Clara." Miriam's recognition disguises itself as a struggle between higher and lower natures:

> So in May she asked him to come to Willey Farm and meet Mrs. Dawes.
> There was something he hankered after. She saw him, whenever they

spoke of Clara Dawes, rouse and get slightly angry. He said he did not like her. Yet he was keen to know about her. Well, he should put himself to the test. She believed that there were in him desires for higher things, and desires for lower, and that the desires for the higher would conquer. At any rate, he should try.

It is a recapitulation of Gertrude Morel's reluctant giving of William to Lily, which constitutes in effect the necessary condition for such a union—the acceptance from the mother's hand of her successor.

When Paul and Clara and Miriam are together, Miriam falls into the role of the Gertrude who disapproves of dancing and of sexual desires. And Paul, treating Miriam exactly as if she were his mother, pantomimically makes his escape: He was utterly unfaithful to her even in her own presence; then he was ashamed, then repentant; then he hated her, and went off again. Those were the ever-recurring conditions."

But Clara, too, is a surrogate mother, the opposite of Gertrude and Miriam, the "harlot," the possession of another. It is from her hands that Paul receives, not the virginal Miriam, but the sexually obtainable Miriam. Before she sleeps with Paul, Clara symbolically introduces Paul to sex. She tells him, in effect, what the real relations between his parents are. Paul insists that Miriam wants only a soul union."

> "How do you know what she is?"
> "I do! I know she wants a sort of soul union."
> "But how do you know what she wants?"
> "I've been with her for seven years."
> "And you haven't found out the first thing about her."
> "What's that?"
> "That she doesn't want any of your soul communion. That's your imagination. She wants you."
> He pondered over this. Perhaps he was wrong.
> "But she seems—" he began.
> "You've never tried," she answered.

"With the spring came again the old madness and battle," starts the next chapter, called "The Test on Miriam." It is full of the imagery of the impenetrable hymen, against which Paul, armed with knowledge, must force himself. There is an "obstacle," "physical bondage," virginity as a "positive force," so "hard to overcome," something Paul must "deliberately break through." Paul fears the "sacrifice" of himself in marriage as "degrading." In giving Paul to Miriam, before taking him herself, Clara is like Queen Gertrude, and Paul like Hamlet. Clara's sexual knowledgeableness inspires Paul to talk to the "nunlike" Miriam of "country matters" for the first time, suggesting that they become lovers. " 'Sometime you will have me?' he murmured [note the passivity of the speaker], hiding his face on her shoulder.

It was so difficult." And when the affair is disastrous, and the "dead" Miriam gives Paul back to Clara, Clara strews Miriam's grave with contempt. She agrees with Gertrude Morel about her. "What I hate is the bloodhound quality in Miriam," she tells Paul's mother, and Paul, angry, yet in agreement with her, buries Miriam forever.

The shift from Miriam to Clara is the shift from *mater urania* to *mater pandemos*. Miriam is the incomplete metamorphosis of the real mother to her unconsciously idealized form. Miriam resembles Gertrude in purity and intellectuality and protectiveness. With Clara the metamorphosis is complete; we can no longer refer her maternal qualities to some real person, but must look to some elemental concept of maternity and orgiastic sexuality as one sees it in the chthonic goddesses, Cybele, Ishtar, Hertha. . . .

Clara fulfills all the conditions Freud describes as proper to her being chosen by Paul. She is the possession of another man, the "injured third party," Baxter Dawes, from whom it seems desirable that Paul "rescue" her. Paul suddenly realizes her vulnerability when they first meet, her need to be rescued: "Suddenly looking at her, he saw that the upward lifting of her face was misery and not scorn. His heart grew tender for everybody. He turned and was gentle with Miriam whom he had neglected till then." In the perfect grasp he has of this sudden reaction there is implicit the further desire by Paul that Clara be a fallen woman, Magdalen, the "harlot." Before this he has recognized her sensual appeal to him. " 'Look at her mouth—made for passion and the very setback of her throat'—He threw his head back in Clara's definite manner."

When Paul visits Clara and sees the shabbiness of her life he is unconsciously excited by the notion of "rescue." . . . Seated at her lacework she seems to Paul a Penelope, waiting. The image is apt, for it is again the waiting mother in need of a rescue, to which Telemachus dedicates himself. Paul sees her also as a "Juno dethroned," a comparison that introduces another remarkable series of descriptive terms applied to Clara. One infallible sign of a divinity, either male or female, according to Greek religious belief, was the slightly larger than human size of the visitant. According to Freudian theory the giants of the world's mythologies originated in the infantile phantasies concerning adults, parents especially, the memories of a time when certain human beings were regularly huge and terrifyingly capable of lifting one up bodily. Shakespeare's Venus—

> Over one arm the lusty courser's rein,
> Under the other was the tender boy—

is the love-enthralled Titan with Adonis. To Clara, Lawrence applies the images of giantism. Paul sees under her clothes "her strong form that seemed to slumber with power." He sees her hand, "large, to match her large limbs," in contrast to his own smaller, delicate hands. He feels her heavy shoulder upon him, her "white, heavy arm." "There was no himself. The grey and black eyes of Clara, her bosom coming down on him. . . . Then he felt himself small and helpless, her towering in her force above him." So in this "composite" imaginary woman Lawrence gathers the attributes of the Great Mother par excellence, "her bosom coming down on him"; what Freud calls "the memory picture of his mother as it has dominated him since the beginning of childhood."

In their sexual intercourse Lawrence carries on the idealizing process, "the way of phantasies." It is a kind of intercourse the real Miriam would not allow him to have, the paradisal situation (Paradise is mentioned) in which there is no consciousness. . . . But underneath the stock vitalism there lurks the same passive yielding that characterized his intercourse with Miriam. The difference lies in the role Clara plays as the "harlot" of phantasy. Freud expands the harlot theme in another essay to explain the phenomenon of psychical impotence in terms of the "incest-barrier" and steps taken to overcome it. One step is to separate the lust object from the love object, i.e., the harlot from the madonna:

> The whole sphere of love in such people remains divided in the two directions personified in art as sacred and profane (or animal) love. Where they love they do not desire and where they desire they cannot love. They seek objects which they do not need to love, in order to keep their sensuality away from the objects they love; and, in accordance with the laws of the "complexive sensitiveness" and of the return of the repressed, the strange failure shown in psychical impotence makes its appearance whenever an object which has been chosen with the aim of avoiding incest recalls the prohibited object through some feature, often an inconspicuous one.
>
> The main protective measure against such a disturbance which men have recourse to in this split in their love consists in a physical *debasement* of the sexual object . . .

In terms of the above-quoted passage Paul's affair with Clara falls within a predictable pattern of behavior, compatible with the other actions of the protagonist. Relieved for the moment, with this beautiful "composite," of the incestuous identification, Paul lapses into the very pleasurable but extremely regressive pleasure of the "nothingness" passion can reduce him to, closely related to the "reaching out to death" of his affair with Miriam. Then, because Clara is, even more than Miriam, the product of an incestuous synthesis, the "return of the repressed" reasserts itself:

> Their loving grew more mechanical, without the marvellous glamour. Gradually they began to introduce novelties to get back some of the feeling of satisfaction. . . . And afterward each of them was rather ashamed,

and these things caused a distance between the two of them. He began to despise her a little, as if she had merited it!

Part of the "debasement" of the object involves, I believe, an element of self-debasement or, if debasement is not the exact term, an attempt to achieve a callousness of sensibility which will make the woman's debasement acceptable. In this case, the refined, sensitive Paul, in the very beginning, which is the most exciting phase of his affair with Clara, lapses into his father's Midland dialect after he has been with Clara on the raw, red, clay bank of the Trent in flood, as if this gross, sexual act had been the *rite de passage* that put him on terms of equality with his father. The brutal natural surroundings, so unlike the soft meadow and pine forest of Miriam's defloration, and the scattered red petals of the carnation, a dream symbol of the menses, speak for the degradation both of the woman into adultery and of the man into the coarser, less sensitive state of manhood. But afterward, as if to reassert his status as the son, Paul, just as he did with Gertrude, insists upon cleaning Clara's boots. The harlot-mother identification is completed. " 'And now I'll clean thy boots and make thee fit for respectable folk,' he said." Paul had cleaned his mother's boots "with as much reverence as if they had been flowers." Not that his mother's shoes needed cleaning. "Mrs. Morel was one of those naturally exquisite people who can walk in mud without dirtying their shoes." In the light of this comparison the boot cleaning becomes a ritual, like the raising of Magdalen to the level of Mary. Gertrude's sexual "shoes" (compare the removal of shoes as a sign of refusal to marry in the Bible in Deuteronomy 25:6) are not dirty, even though she has borne children. Clara's shoes, after her intercourse with Paul, must be cleaned. The act raises her to the status of mother as well as mistress. Freud points out the fetichism connected with the foot as a very primitive sexual symbol and notes the aptness of the shoe as a symbol for the female genitals. . . .

With the dying of Paul's mother, Paul's sexuality begins to equate itself more and more with actual death. Like Dostoevsky's epileptic seizures, whose psychogenic origin Freud founds in a pantomime of his father's death, Paul's orgasm in Clara's arms is a little death.

. . . He wanted her—he had her—and it made her feel as if death itself had her in its grip. She lay in horror.

With Paul's last embrace of a living woman all three women are finally joined and identified as one, the mother. When she dies, the regressive, incestuous phantasies her life had fed sicken and die with her. The pleasantly deathly consummation with Miriam and the Nirvana-like "impersonality of passion" with Clara resolve themselves in Paul's horror at the coldness of his mother's lips, a horror he inverts and feels in Clara when he lies with her. Gertrude's death releases both Clara and Miriam from their functions as mother surrogates. They do not die for Paul: it is he, finally, who samples death, first pantomiming it in Clara's arms and, at the last, feeling it on his mother's mouth. Clara's horror of him is based on this: that Paul is trying to "die" on her.

In the end Paul rejects death; *Sons and Lovers* is a comedy of the Oedipus complex. He is not Oedipus standing on the steps of his stricken house—he is journeying forth. Even the blindness is touched upon. Paul is described as turning "blindly." "He dared not meet his own eyes in the mirror. He never looked at himself." But the rejection of death is positive and absolute, and in its rejection, perverse as it may seem, is the implicit rejection, valid in unconscious terms, of the women to whom he might have turned after the long night of his childhood was past. By rejecting Miriam and Clara, Paul dramatically represents to himself the profound change that has come over him. Fiction is invoked to dispel what in real life might have been an attenuating relationship, and to put in its place a more dramatic *hic incipit vita nova.*

When Miriam, out of compassion, asks him to marry her, his reply shows the extent of his knowledge of what has happened. "But—you love me so much, you want to put me in your pocket. And I should die there, smother." The unconscious formulation of the reply is rather an expression on Paul's part of his refusal to be tempted to crawl into another pocket, now that the one he has been in for so long has worn out and left him free.

It is Paul's walk, on the last page of *Sons and Lovers*, toward the "faintly humming, glowing town" that sounds the note of positive choice. And the choice is, in psychoanalytic terms, a classically important one. In choosing the town Paul is accepting his father, an idealized image, like Hamlet's father, a "man," with all the expansive attributes the generic term allows. Turning his back upon his home place he is rejecting, or at least modifying, his acceptance of the mother. I think the process can be described as an inversion, a turning over to find a new center of gravity, long withheld. Whereas before Paul had, in the mother, loved an idealized image, capable of dangerous extensions into mother surrogates like Miriam and Clara, he had, in the father, hated (with that curious ambivalence, already noted) an identity, with a local habitation and a name. With Baxter Dawes, the process begins to reverse itself. The father's identity begins to be idealized and lose its historical boundaries in Walter Morel, while Gertrude Morel is forced, by the exigencies of Paul's insistence upon becoming a man, into mere motherhood; and with this her surrogates lose their vitality and fall away.

From the very beginning the town stands in polar hostility to Gertrude, as the world of men, of deflowered countryside. It is to the town that Walter Morel and Jerry Purdy take their pub-crawling walk. The "wakes" is a part of town life, the first sounds, for young William Morel, of the outside world: "the braying of a merry-go-round and the tooting of a horn." Gertrude hates the wakes, and Lawrence describes William, crucified by a choice, who "stood watching her, cut to the heart to let her go, and yet unable to leave the wakes." For Paul in his turn the town exercises its attraction: "From the train going home at night he used to watch the lights of the town, sprinkled thick on the hills, fusing together in a blaze in the valleys. He felt rich in life and happy." Like the "stars and sun, a few bright grains . . . holding each other in embrace," the town defies the dark, sometimes horrible, onetime appeal of the maternal invitation to be still and passive. It is, like all the towers, citadels, mountaintops, and Beautiful Cities of Literature, the place to which one fights his way through the seas and jungles of world or mind.

In the end of *Sons and Lovers* is implicit an acceptance of the father's values. Oedipus says, in what is the essential irony of the play: "In doing right by Laius I protected myself, for whoever slew Laius might turn a hand against me." Paul Morel is categorically rejecting all the elements of his Oedipal involvement. Having restored the Player King, Baxter Dawes, to his Player Queen, Clara, he enters the town, a man both driven and drawn across the threshold into manhood. In ratifying finally the bents and needs of the father, he "protects" himself.

Sons and Lovers

by Keith Sagar

[Lawrence's account of the theme of *Sons and Lovers,* sent to Edward Garnett in the well-known letter of November 14, 1912] has elicited almost unqualified approval.[1] If this were offered as an analysis of Lawrence's own experience as he then saw it, we could not demur. That it should be offered, however, as the "idea" which *Sons and Lovers* follows, and as evidence that the novel "has got form —*form*: haven't I made it patiently, out of sweat as well as blood," means that, testing it against the novel we have, we can only find it located and misleading. Certainly it bears no resemblance to Jessie Chambers's account of the novel ("a slander—a fearful treachery"):

> In *Sons and Lovers* Lawrence handed his mother the laurels of victory . . .

> I realised that the entire structure of the story rested upon the attitude he had adopted. To do any kind of justice to our relationship would involve a change in his attitude towards his mother's influence, and of that I was now convinced he was incapable.

Lawrence's 1912 account is of the novel he might then have written —not the novel we have:

> I would write a different *Sons and Lovers* now; my mother was wrong, and I thought she was absolutely right. (Frieda Lawrence, *Not I But the Wind* 52.)

Right or wrong as Lydia Lawrence may have been, Gertrude Morel is right, though the novel qualifies her rightness—it is not absolute, but relative to the alternatives which are offered. And, as Jessie Chambers observes, it is this attitude towards her which determines "the entire structure of the story." The novel does not attribute the split in Paul's consciousness to his mother's possessiveness and jealousy; nor does it present the failure of the two love-affairs as a "neurotic

---

"Sons and Lovers." *From* The Art of D. H. Lawrence, *by Keith Sagar (Cambridge: Cambridge University Press, 1966), pp. 21–35. Reprinted with the author's revisions by permission of the publisher.*

[1] [Excerpts from Lawrence's letter are reprinted in this volume, pp. 86–87.]

refusal of life" ([Graham] Hough, *The Dark Sun* 42) engendered in him by his parents' failure.

Morel is held responsible for his own collapse ("he had denied the God in him"). . . . But it does not follow that Mrs. Morel must be in the tradition of destructive women. . . . There is a destructive element in her relations with both husband and sons; but the over-riding impression is of a normality and strength of character which serves as a standard against which the other women in the novel are judged, and found wanting.

II

The talk was lively and Mrs. Lawrence seemed to be the pivot on which the liveliness centred. She struck me as a bright, vivacious little woman, full of vitality, and amusingly emphatic in her way of speaking.

This was Jessie Chambers's impression of Mrs Lawrence, before the "little woman" became her rival. And it is in just these terms—liveli-ness, brightness, vivaciousness, vitality—that she dominates *Sons and Lovers* and takes on a pivotal significance in its structure.

It is this same vitality in Morel which draws Gertrude Coppard to him:

He was full of colour and animation, his voice ran into comic grotesque, he was so ready and so pleasant with everybody. . . . He danced well, as if it were natural and joyous in him to dance.

This, for her, is manhood, contrasting with her own earnestness, with her father's puritanism, with the lack of manliness in her former suitor, John Field, who had allowed his father to browbeat him into business when he wanted to enter the clergy. . . . In Walter Morel, she seeks to complete herself, to achieve fulfilment, through marriage:

The next Christmas they were married, and for three months she was perfectly happy: for six months she was very happy.

But the happiness continues to dwindle. "There was nothing at the back of all his show."

Sometimes, when she herself wearied of love-talk, she tried to open her heart seriously to him. She saw him listen deferentially, but without un-derstanding. This killed her efforts at a finer intimacy, and she had flashes of fear. Sometimes he was restless of an evening: it was not enough for him just to be near her, she realised.

He drifts back to his drinking, and begins to ill-treat her.

There began a battle between them the husband and wife—a fearful, bloody battle that ended only with the death of one. She fought to make

him undertake his responsibilities, to make him fulfil his obligations. But
he was too different from her. His nature was purely sensuous, and she
strove to make him moral, religious. She tried to force him to face things.
He could not endure it—it drove him out of his mind.

Mrs. Morel's religion is presented here not as chapel-going, but as a
moral obligation to face reality, to be responsible for one's life, to
have integrity. She does not merely make impossible demands of
Morel. She goes more than half-way to meet him. She accepts the
squalor and poverty. She is a model housewife and mother. She sees
in Mr. Leivers a man who would have let her help him. Even little
Barker is "ten times the man" Morel is. Through irresponsibility he
forfeits his health. He loses the energy even to quarrel and bully, and,
when Mrs. Morel dies, is left a pathetic lifeless figure. Even if we feel
that her demands *were* impossible; that Morel *could* not become responsible, he is not to be forgiven in Lawrence's strictly existential
morality: "for the real tragedy went on in Morel in spite of himself."
He is even responsible for his accidents in the pit. . . . "Everything
deep in him he denied." It is from his own vital core which is God
in him, that fate emanates. . . . Morel lingers on at the end of *Sons
and Lovers* adrift even from his own tragedy.

Mrs. Morel turns to her sons, but not for sterile compensation. She
gives always more than she receives. It is not until she is dying that
she begins to sap Paul's life. For, despite the tragedy of her marriage,
she has not been broken. Indeed she has salvaged from the early
days something of immense and lasting value:

> "My Mother, I believe, got real joy and satisfaction out of my father at
> first. I believe she had a passion for him; that's why she stayed with
> him," [Paul said]. . . . There's not a tiny bit of feeling of sterility about
> her. . . .

In the early chapters we see Paul being kindled to life by his
mother. They have ecstatic excursions to Nottingham and Lincoln.
The words "jolly" and "gay" figure prominently. In such scenes the
brightness and love is realised largely through naturalistic dialogue.
Sometimes it is more concentrated, and poetic:

> Once roused, he opened his eyes to see his mother standing on the hearth-
> rug with the hot iron near her cheek, listening, as it were, to the heat.
> Her still face, with the mouth closed tight from suffering and disillusion
> and self-denial, and her nose the smallest bit on one side, and her blue
> eyes so young, quick, and warm made his heart contract with love. When
> she was quiet, so, she looked brave and rich with life. . . .
>
> Her movements were light and quick. It was always a pleasure to watch
> her. Nothing she ever did, no movement she ever made, could have been
> found fault with by her children. The room was warm and full of the
> scent of hot linen.

Young, quick, warm, brave, rich, life—these words have their effect. The warmth has its source in Mrs. Morel's eyes as much as in the fire-light and the hot linen. And the quickness of her eyes and movements (controlled by a central poise and stillness) uses the alternative meaning of the word to convey life itself ("the quick and the dead"). It is significant that the last word of the novel is "quickly."

III

The second third of the novel is concerned largely with Miriam, though Mrs. Morel's presence is always felt. Gradually Paul comes to mediate between Miriam and life. Miriam lives through her soul. She finds difficulty in assimilating sensuous experience.

> And she was cut off from ordinary life by her religious intensity which made the world for her either a nunnery garden or a paradise, where sin and knowledge were not, or else an ugly, cruel thing. . . .

It is Mrs. Morel who first notices that Miriam is pulling the heart out of Paul. Gradually it becomes clear that it is this "absorption" by Miriam which is causing the "split" in Paul's consciousness, not any demands made by his mother:

> With Miriam he was always on the high plane of abstraction, when his natural fire of love was transmitted into the fine stream of thought. . . .
> Then, if she put her arm in his, it caused him almost torture. . . .

And the frustration which this "split" causes becomes more and more clearly sexual:

> The fact that he might want her as a man wants a woman had in him been suppressed into a shame. . . .

At last he breaks with Miriam and writes a valedictory letter to her:

> See, you are a nun. I have given you what I would give a holy nun. . . . That is why we cannot love in the common sense. . . . If people marry, they must live together as affectionate humans, who may be common place with each other without feeling awkward—not as two souls.

Miriam's abnormality is related to her mother, just as Paul's relative normality is to his. Early in the relationship there is evident a serious maladjustment in both mother and daughter, towards the realities of farm life:

> Miriam was exceedingly sensitive, as her mother had always been. . . .
> It could never be mentioned that the mare was in foal.

The placing of the last sentence establishes that the failure towards Paul is only one manifestation of a general failure towards life.

Miriam idealises love to purify it from "the faintest suggestion of
such intercourse." Otherwise "she felt as if her whole soul coiled into
knots of shame." She prays "make me love him—as Christ would,
who died for the souls of men." All this prepares us for the ultimate
failure, when Paul goes back to Miriam to try to break down her
spirituality through a physical consummation, and achieves, instead,
only a ritual slaughter:

> Her big brown eyes were watching him, still and resigned and loving;
> she lay as if she had given herself up to sacrifice: there was her body for
> him; but the look at the back of her eyes, like a creature awaiting
> immolation, arrested him, and all his blood fell back. . . .

It is the dead hand of the mother once more upon Miriam:

> "Mother said to me: There is one thing in marriage that is always dread-
> ful, but you have to bear it. And I believed it."

IV

The unnatural intensity, the clenched will of Miriam, relates her unmistakably to Hermione Roddice of *Women in Love,* even in its physical manifestation, a heaviness, almost a clumsiness in her movements:

> Her body was not flexible and living. She walked with a swing, rather
> heavily, her head bowed forward, pondering. She was not clumsy, and
> yet none of her movements seemed quite *the* movement. . . . There was
> no looseness or abandon about her. . . .

We are reminded again of Mrs. Morel:

> Her movements were light and quick. It was always a pleasure to watch
> her. Nothing she ever did, no movement she ever made, could have been
> found fault with by her children.

But, even more than it throws us back to Mrs. Morel, this throws us
forward to Clara:

> She stood on top of the stile, and he held both hands. Laughing, she
> looked down into his eyes. Then she leaped. Her breast came against his;
> he held her, and covered her face with kisses.

The Miriam passage continues:

> But she was physically afraid. If she were getting over a stile, she gripped
> his hands in a little hard anguish, and began to lose her presence of
> mind. And he could not persuade her to jump from even a small height.
> Her eyes dilated, became exposed and palpitating. "No!" she cried, half
> laughing in terror—"no!". . .

The same physical inhibition prevents Miriam from enjoying the
swing. This episode is characteristic of the novel—remarkable for its

realism and freshness, embodying resources far greater than those needed for mere presentation, resources which serve to relate the episode closely to the overall structure of the novel and to invest it with a deeper moral significance.

Paul swings "like a bird that swings for joy of movement"; he finds it "a treat of a swing—a real treat of a swing." Miriam is amazed that he takes his enjoyment so seriously. But for Paul life is made up of such moments of intensity, an intensity as relaxed and whole as hers is taut and unbalanced, moments when the body is given over to something outside the will, in this case the rhythm of the swing:

> She could feel him falling and lifting through the air, as if he were lying on some force . . . For the moment he was nothing but a piece of swinging stuff: not a particle of him that did not swing.

Miriam is roused watching him:

> It were almost as if he were a flame that had lit a warmth in her whilst he swung in the middle air.

Mrs. Morel had been able to yield to joy, to Walter's "flame of life," but Miriam "cannot lose herself so." When her turn comes she grips the rope with fear, resisting the forces which seek to carry her. The sexual implication is clear in the hot waves of fear through her bowels which accompany Paul's rhythmic thrusts. The fiasco of their eventual consummation could be predicted from this scene.

Miriam's reluctance to give herself up to life, and, more specifically, to put herself in the hands of the man she loves, contrasts, again, with Clara. . . . Clara's natural abandon makes their first intimacy easy for Paul, despite the hazards. Afterwards, glowing with happiness, they go for tea in the village. An old lady presents Clara with "three tiny dahlias in full blow, neat as bees, and speckled scarlet and white." The offering is made "because we were jolly," Paul tells Miriam.

Flower themes are woven into the whole novel so skilfully that only cumulatively does one recognise their symbolism. A scene in the first chapter identifies Mrs. Morel with the flowers, and, through them, with all the mysterious potentialities of life. . . . She is pregnant with Paul, and it is stressed that this communion [with nature] is shared by the unborn child. The night she looks out on is not only nature, it is all that the infinite distance offers:

> The night was very large, and very strange, stretching its hoary distances infinitely. And out of the silver-grey fog of darkness came sounds vague and hoarse: a corncrake not far off, sound of a train like a sigh, and distant shouts of men.

The symbolic character of the passage is underlined on the following page, when Mrs. Morel, looking in the mirror, smiles to see "her face all smeared with the yellow dust of lilies." The night into which Mrs.

Morel here merges is moonlit, shiny, hoary, silver-grey, rich with scents and sounds and the dusky gold of the pollen. And Paul is here baptised into life.

At the structural centre of the novel, at the critical moment when Paul rejects Miriam finally for Clara, there is a second night-communion which in part repeats, in part subtly qualifies and extends, the symbolism of the first. The lilies are now described as madonna lilies:

> Through the open door, stealthily, came the scent of madonna lilies, almost as if it were prowling abroad.

We remember from the earlier scene the overpowering perfume, the streaming white light of the full moon, the whiteness of all the flowers. In the later scene there is a half-moon, dusky gold, which makes the sky dull purple, and which disappears below the hill at the very moment when Paul catches "another perfume, something raw and coarse":

> Hunting round, he found the purple iris, touched their fleshy throats and their dark, grasping hands. At any rate he had found something.

The next chapter is called "Passion." The intense whiteness of the full moon and the lilies, formerly a condition of Paul's growth within an all-encompassing mother-love, is now becoming a weight upon him, a "barrier" to his further maturing. The blanched white light is the possession of his soul by women who, as mother and virgin, cannot foster the life of the body and the development of a strong, self-sufficient masculinity.

As the first night-communion gave a blessing to the unborn child, so the second blesses the new self which is coming into being within Paul:

> Often, as he talked to Clara Dawes, came that thickening and quickening of his blood, that peculiar concentration in the breast, as if something were alive there, a new self, or a new centre of consciousness.

The new self responds to Clara impersonally, as a woman rather than a person, almost physiologically. And Mrs. Morel approves: "At any rate that feeling was wholesome." . . . [Yet] Mrs. Morel's verdict is confirmed by the novel:

> Yes, I liked her. But you'll tire of her my son; you know you will.

The consummation with Clara is wonderfully done. . . . The abstraction of his relationship with Miriam—"his natural fire of love . . . transmitted into the fine stream of thought"—had cut him off from life. Clara puts him in touch again:

> Just as he was, so it seemed the vigorous wintry stars were strong also with life. He and they struck with the same pulse of fire, and the same

joy of strength which held the bracken-frond stiff near his eyes held his own body firm.

Throughout the novel, this faculty for being in touch with life has been stressed in Paul, and its absence in Miriam. It is a matter of respect for the unique otherness of phenomena, the mythic faculty of meeting phenomena in an I–thou relationship, meeting but not merging, as Miriam seeks to do, which is a violation of individuality. Sexual union with Clara is not at all a merging of identities. It is through the very strangeness of the woman that Paul gains access to the darkness which is both the unknown forces and purposes deep within himself. . . . From now on in Lawrence's work, life is not to be judged by merely human standards; rather, human values are themselves exposed to standards drawn from experiences and relationships in an animistic universe:

> To know their own nothingness, to know the tremendous living flood which carried them always, gave them rest within themselves. If so great a magnificent power could overwhelm them, identify them altogether with itself, so that they knew that they were only grains in the tremendous heave that lifted every grass blade its little height, and every tree, and living thing, then why fret about themselves? They could let themselves be carried by life, and they felt a sort of peace, each in the other. There was a verification which they had had together. Nothing could nullify it, nothing could take it away; it was almost their belief in life.

It is this faith which finally saves Paul from the temptation to merge with the dying mother into the other darkness, of death. Clara has now taken over from the mother the initiation of Paul into life.

[But the imagery of the Trent in flood, which conveys the significance of Paul's passion for Clara,] has also suggested the limitations of this passion; like floodwaters, it is something beyond control, accumulated and unresolved, unless it takes its place in a whole human relationship which Paul finds impossible with Clara.

I cannot see what prevents a permanent relationship between Paul and Clara. The ease with which they are so shortly to separate leaves rather high and dry these powerful affirmative passages. I would not be surprised to find that these passages were new in the final, 1912 version and drew their power from Lawrence's relationship with Frieda. Lawrence was probably strongly tempted to make Clara into a Frieda figure, but realized that the novel as it stood could not accommodate such potent new material, but must end with the death of the mother and Paul alone in the world. It might have been better for the unity of the novel if the lovemaking with Clara had yielded intimations rather than such confident affirmations of life.

V

After the failure with Clara, Paul begins to doubt his capacity for loving any woman other than his mother.

> "You haven't met the right woman."
> "And I never shall meet the right woman while you live," he said.
> She was very quiet. Now she began to feel tired, as if she were done.

Mrs. Morel has up to this point supplied Paul with the standards with which to judge both Miriam and Clara and find them wanting. But he is unable to separate the moral qualities for which his mother stands (and which the novel never calls in question) from her actual physical presence and his close filial relationship with her. But it is in terms of those very standards that the relationship is now seen to be retarding. If Paul continues to lean on his mother and live through her, he will never discover whether he has succeeded in incorporating her strengths into his own character. Unless he can learn to live without daily reference to her and dependence on her, no complete relationship with another woman will be possible for him, nor will he be able to survive his mother's death. Without her the night which she had made him a part of, containing all the un-realised potentialities of life (its sights and sounds had "roused" and "invigorated" Mrs. Morel), becomes not the womb of day, but its winding sheet:

> The town . . . stretched away over the bay of railway, a level fume of lights. Beyond the town, the country, little smouldering spots for more towns—the sea—the night—on and on! And he had no place in it! . . . Everywhere the vastness and terror of the immense night which is roused and stirred for a brief while by the day, but which returns, and will remain at last eternal, holding everything in its silence and living gloom.

Paul's will fights to voice his mother's values against his own temptation to follow "in the wake of his beloved":

> "You've got to keep alive for her sake," said his will in him. . . . "You've got to carry forward her living, and what she had done, go on with it."

He turns, at the end, to seek for life in new places:

> But no, he would not give in. Turning sharply, he walked towards the city's gold phosphorescence. His fists were shut, his mouth set fast. He would not take that direction, to follow her. He walked towards the faintly humming, glowing town, quickly.

"The city's gold phosphorescence" beckons, like the "dusky gold" of Morel's youthful flame of life, like the pollen and the half-moon, towards the unknown—full of richness and the promise of life.

Counterfeit Loves

by Mark Spilka

Sons and Lovers is interpreted, much too often, in terms of the "split" theory which Lawrence once outlined in a letter to Edward Garnett.[1] According to that letter, William and Paul Morel are unable to love normally when they come to manhood, because their dominant mother holds them back, so that a split occurs between body and soul—their sweethearts getting the former; their mother, the latter; while the boys themselves are shattered, inwardly, in the course of the struggle.

Admittedly, this theory accounts for much of the surface tension of the novel; but as Mark Schorer has pointed out, it seems to conflict with a second and wholly different scheme of motivation. Unless I am badly mistaken, this second scheme is more important than the first. For there seem to be *two* psychologies at work in *Sons and Lovers,* one imposed upon the other, though without destroying its effectiveness. We know, for example, that Lawrence had heard about Freud before he wrote the final draft of the novel.[2] We also know that the Garnett letter refers to the final draft, and that previous versions of the book had followed somewhat different lines. So

[1] The letter is quoted and approved by Horace Gregory in *Pilgrim of the Apocalypse* and by Harry Moore in *The Life and Works of D. H. Lawrence.* It forms the basis of Mark Schorer's rather sharp attack on the novel, in "Technique as Discovery." Scraps and fragments of it appear in other studies, in the general effort to bolster purely Freudian readings of the novel. . . . As a number of critics have noted, there is at least one obvious discrepancy between the letter and the novel: at the end, Miriam takes the drift toward death, and Paul turns away from it. [Lawrence's letter to Garnett appears on pp. 86–87 of this volume. An excerpt from Mark Schorer's "Technique as Discovery" is reprinted on pp. 97–99.]

[2] In *Freudianism and the Literary Mind,* Frederick Hoffman quotes Frieda Lawrence to the effect that she and Lawrence had long arguments about Freud while Lawrence was preparing the final draft of *Sons and Lovers.* Hoffman suggests that these discussions led Lawrence to increase the emphasis upon the mother-son relationship, "to the neglect of other matters," but he feels that the book was "only superficially affected" by Lawrence's introduction to Freud (p. 153).

Lawrence may well have written the book, at first, in accord with his own developing psychology, and then rewritten it in garbled accord with Freud's: hence the confusion, and the effect of superimposition, which bothers Mr. Schorer and many other readers. But if this is so, then the novel takes its strength from Lawrence's psychology and its weakness (inadvertently) from Freud's. The "split" theory, for example, is more Freudian than Laurentian; it involves a kind of Freudian triangle—mother-son-sweetheart—while the conflict in all future novels centers upon a single man and woman, a specific couple, whose relationship is judged or resolved in terms of its own vitality. We have already seen such conflicts, incidentally, in the floral scenes in *Sons and Lovers,* where vitality, or the full glow of the life-flame, is the chief criterion in Paul's specific relations with his mother, and with Miriam and Clara—where each affair is judged, in other words, in terms of its effect upon the life-flow, or the "livingness," of the man and woman involved. And as a matter of fact, each of Paul's three loves is actually significant in itself, since each contributes something vital to his development, yet finally proves destructive and inadequate. So all three loves—spiritual, oedipal, and possessive—resemble the counterfeit loves of later stories, and this in spite of the obvious Freudian twist which Lawrence seems to give them in his final draft.

Romantic Miriam Leivers, for example, with her love of intellect, her heavy dumb will, and her attempt to abstract the soul right out of Paul's body, has something in common with Hermione Roddice, that harsh creature of will and intellect in *Women in Love.* There is common ground, too, between what Clara Dawes wants out of Paul—possession, imprisoning personal love—and the princess-slave relationship in later stories like "The Captain's Doll." In the same vein, Mrs. Morel resembles the later and less appealing mothers in Lawrence's short stories (say, Pauline Attenborough in "The Lovely Lady," or Rachel Bodoin in "Mother and Daughter") who sap the life from their children, regardless of outside competition, because oedipal love is sterile in itself. The truth is, then, that *Sons and Lovers* is mainly an exploration of destructive or counterfeit loves—with a garbled Freudian "split" imposed upon it. At least this helps to explain the unique emotional tenor of the book: for in spite of all confusion there is a strange new reading experience here, a unique event in the realm of fiction, and in the realm of morality as well. Indeed, if *Sons and Lovers* is (as Harry Moore tells us) "the last novel of the nineteenth century," it is also one of the first novels of the twentieth. The book is only outwardly conventional;[3] it draws its

[3] One of the most deceptive aspects of the book, for example, is its apparent use of the class structure of the mining community as the realistic framework for the novel. This is in strict accord with nineteenth-century tradition. But except for the Leivers family, the members of the local community are only lightly sketched in. So the real framework for the novel becomes the Morel family itself, with Paul at its center: hence the book's original title, *Paul Morel. . . .*

greatest strength from Lawrence's radical new insight, moral as well as psychological, into the complex nature of emotional conflict.

II

Jessie Chambers cites a number of significant lines which appeared in the first draft of *Sons and Lovers,* but which were eliminated in the final version:

> "What was it he (Paul Morel) wanted of her (Miriam)? Did he want her to break his mother down in him? Was that what he wanted?"
>
> And again: "Mrs. Morel saw that if Miriam could only win her son's sex sympathy there would be nothing left for her." (*D. H. Lawrence: A Personal Record,* p. 191)

In the final draft of the book, and in Lawrence's letter to Garnett, this conflict is *stated* somewhat differently: if Miriam should win Paul's *soul,* then there would be nothing left for Mrs. Morel; as for his sex sympathy, the mother wants her to win that, if she will only leave his soul in her possession. Yet Lawrence makes it perfectly clear, through dramatic portions of the book, that Miriam's failure to attract Paul, physically, has led to her defeat in the spiritual conflict, and we see at once that the excised lines hold true to the actual situation. The girl's sexual failure is deeply rooted, for example, in her own emotional make-up. As Lawrence amply demonstrates, she is unable to lose herself in any simple pleasurable occasion, her body is tense and lifeless, her abnormal spiritual intensity is coupled with a genuine fear of things physical:

> She walked with a swing, rather heavily, her head bowed forward, pondering. She was not clumsy, and yet none of her movements seemed quite *the* movement. Often, when wiping the dishes, she would stand in bewilderment and chagrin because she had pulled in two halves a cup or a tumbler. It was as if, in her fear and self-mistrust, she put too much strength into the effort. There was no looseness or abandon about her. Everything was gripped stiff with intensity, and her effort, over-charged, closed in on itself. . . .

Lawrence even suggests the future sexual problem, in an early scene, when Miriam shows Paul the swing in her father's barn. Characteristically, she sacrifices the first turn to him, and he flies through the air, "every bit of him swinging, like a bird that swoops for joy of movement." Then he turns the swing over to the reluctant girl, and begins to set her in motion.

> She felt the accuracy with which he caught her, exactly at the right moment, and the exactly proportionate strength of his thrust, and she was afraid. Down to her bowels went the hot wave of fear. She was in his hands. Again, firm and inevitable came the thrust at the right mo-

ment. She gripped the rope, almost swooning.

"Ha!" she laughed in fear. "No higher!"

"But you're not a *bit* high," he remonstrated.

"But no higher."

He heard the fear in her voice, and desisted. Her heart melted in hot pain when the moment came for him to thrust her forward again. But he left her alone. She began to breathe.

Yet both Paul and Miriam are prudes in their early courtship. She recoils from "the continual business of birth and begetting" on the farm, and he takes his cue from her. Their own friendship is always pitched, moreover, at an intensely spiritual and intellectual level, so that even the simplest contact seems repellent: "His consciousness seemed to split. The place where she was touching him ran hot with friction. He was one internecine battle, and he became cruel to her because of it." Again, when the two chaste lovers are out for a walk one night, Paul suddenly stands transfixed at the sight of an enormous orange moon; his blood concentrates "like a flame in his chest," but this time Miriam shrinks away from actual contact: "it was as if she could scarcely stand the shock of physical love, even a passionate kiss, and then he was too shrinking and sensitive to give it."

Thus the chief "split" between Paul and Miriam comes from the abstract nature of their love, and not from the mother's hold upon the young man's soul. And the final responsibility for this split belongs with Miriam. When the friendship between the young couple wanes, for example, Paul resigns himself to the old love for his mother. But in the spring of his twenty-third year, he returns to the girl for another try at sensual love. This time, he seeks "the great hunger and impersonality of passion" with her, and though she agrees to this, she decides to submit herself religiously, as if to a sacrifice. Even as their love-making becomes more frequent, she continues to clench herself for the "sacrifice," as she had clenched herself on the swing in earlier days. So the lovers part once more, with this final confirmation that Miriam's frigidity is rooted in her own nature, and not in mere ignorance of sex. Her purity is nullity rather than innocence; she lacks real warmth, and Paul, in his youthful inexperience, is unable to rouse it in her. Although they meet again, after his mother's death, they are still divided by her incompleteness. Paul is shattered and adrift toward death himself; he wants her to respond to him out of warmth, out of womanly instinct. But she merely offers the old familar sacrifice, and Paul rejects it: "he did not hope to give life to her by denying his own."

Yet if Miriam lacks warmth, she has strength of will to spare. She endures Paul's insults, his cruel probings, his wrongheaded arguments; she lets him go, time and again, out of the conviction that she holds the ultimate key to his soul. And she does have the ability to stimulate him in his work, to arouse his own spiritual nature to fever pitch, and to serve as the necessary "threshing floor" for his ideas. Because of this ability, she believes "he cannot do without her"; but her belief results in a significant lapse—a kind of self-betrayal—when Paul decides to break away: "Always—it has always been so," she cries out. "It has been one long battle between us—you fighting away from me." The statement shocks Paul profoundly; he reasons that if she had known this all along, and had said nothing, then their love "had been monstrous."

> He was full of a feeling that she had deceived him. She had despised him when he thought she worshipped him. She had let him say wrong things, and had not contradicted him. She had let him fight alone. . . . All these years she had treated him as if he were a hero, and thought of him secretly as an infant, a foolish child. . . .

The exposure of this duplicity (contempt disguised by reverence) shows Miriam in her truest colors. Quite plainly she resembles the willful Hermione Roddice of *Women in Love,* though she is never so poised, skillful, and predatory as Hermione. But the heavy dumb will is undeniably there, and this, coupled with her fierce desire to be a man, to succeed through intellectual knowledge, makes her a decided forerunner of those feminine creatures of intellect and will whom Lawrence would later deplore as spiritual vampires. Thus Miriam is a nun, in Paul's eyes, who would reduce the world to a nunnery garden: on the one hand, her excessive spirituality smothers his spirit; on the other, it destroys her own capacity to respond, sympathetically, to his newly-awakened need for sensual love.[4] And so she defeats herself in the struggle for Paul's heart, by thwarting his deep male instinct to be loved, impersonally, as a man, rather than

---

[4] This concentrated attention on the lack of balance in Miriam's make-up (and its destructive consequences) seems to be the first clear-cut example of the psychology of organic being, or the "centers-of-consciousness" theory, which Lawrence would later work out, schematically, in *Psychoanalysis and the Unconscious.* The theory is a complicated one, but it does help to clarify the confused relationship between Paul and Miriam, so I will include a fuller explanation of it at this point. Lawrence divides the body into two upper spiritual poles and two lower sensual poles: at each of the two levels there is a positive outward flow of sympathy and a negative assertion of will (the upper "will" achieves objective awareness of the beloved, while the lower "will" asserts the self). Now Miriam functions mainly on her upper poles, so that the flow of her spiritual sympathy tends to be excessive, or stifling, and her upper will is used for predatory ends. In the meantime, she has withered at the sensual level; she has no outward sensual flow (no warmth), nor can she assert her sensual independence (her proud womanhood): hence her touch proves sterile, and she can only feed upon Paul's vitality. All this should be taken figuratively, I think, as a coherent description of subjective human interchange. The scheme was derived *from* the novels, and it functions in them with remarkable flexibility.

as a mind or soul or personality. And she loses to Paul's mother by
default, but she is not really defeated, at the deepest level of the
conflict, by Mrs. Morel.

III

Nor is Clara Dawes defeated by Paul's mother, though she fits in
better with the older woman's plans: she takes care of Paul's sexual
needs, that is, and leaves plenty of him over for Mrs. Morel. So the
mother is "not hostile to the idea of Clara"; in fact, she finds the relationship rather wholesome, after the soul-sucking affair with Miriam.
She even likes Clara, but judges her as somehow not large enough to
hold her son. Paul reaches a similar verdict about his mistress, in-
dependently, when he gives her back to her husband. But since
Clara brings him a potentially fuller love than either Miriam or his
mother, we must examine her role in the book with special care.
She is, after all, the first imperfect version of the Laurentian woman,
the "lost girl" in search of true womanhood.

Paul is 23 when he meets Clara, and she is about 30. He responds
at once to her slumbering warmth, and senses that her aloofness is
just a defensive pose. For her part, Clara admires his animal quickness: he brings her the promise of renewed vitality, and they draw
close together and make love, once Paul has broken away from
Miriam. Thus Paul receives the impersonal love he needs, "the real,
real flame of feeling through another person," and Clara comes to
full awakening as a woman. We can almost feel this transformation,
for example, in a scene which follows their initial consummation in
Clifton Grove. Now the lovers enter Clifton village, take tea at the
house of an old lady, and rouse her to gaiety through their special
warmth. As they are about to leave, the woman comes forward timidly
"with three tiny dahlias in full blow, neat as bees, and speckled
scarlet and white."

> She stood before Clara, pleased with herself, saying:
> "I don't know whether—" and holding the flowers forward in her
> old hand.
> "Oh, how pretty!" cried Clara, accepting the flowers.
> "Shall she have them all?" asked Paul reproachfully of the old woman.
> "Yes, she shall have them all," she replied, beaming with joy. "You
> have got enough for your share."
> "Ah, but I shall ask her to give me one!" he teased.
> "Then she does as she pleases," said the old lady, smiling. And she
> bobbed a little curtsey of delight.

As her delight would seem to indicate, this is a communion scene,
and one which neatly affirms the inward change in both of the lovers.

The reward of flowers, the life-symbol, to Clara is significant enough; but it is the "true and vivid relationship" with the old woman—her bright response to the lovers' mutual warmth—which gives us an immediate sense of inward change. "By life," writes Lawrence, "we mean something that gleams, that has the fourth-dimensional quality" (*Phoenix,* p. 529).

In the months that follow, this "gleam" or fourth-dimensional quality informs the relations between Paul and Clara. When he pins berries on her coat, she watches his quick hands, "and it seemed to her she had never *seen* anything before. Till now, everything had been indistinct." When he embraces her, she feels glad, erect, and proud again: "It was her restoration and her recognition." She falls passionately in love with him, and he with her ("as far as passion went"), till their love becomes an actual immersion in the "fourth dimension." One night, for instance, they take each other in an open field:

> It was all so much bigger than themselves that he was hushed. They had met, and included in their meeting the thrust of the manifold grass-stems, the cry of the peewit, the wheel of the stars. . . .
> And after such an evening, they were both very still, having known the immensity of passion. . . .
> They could let themselves be carried by life, and they felt a sort of peace each in the other. There was a verification which they had had together. Nothing could nullify it, nothing could take it away; it was almost their belief in life.

Later on, Lawrence drops the "almost" out of that final phrase, and develops his belief in life from sexual love, or from the connection with the life-force which sexual love implies. But in *Sons and Lovers,* his belief has barely taken shape, and the conflict between Paul and Clara is never well-defined. Nevertheless, the lines of definition are there, and Lawrence makes good use of them. Thus Clara is soon dissatisfied with impersonal love; like Miriam, she wants to grasp hold of Paul and to possess him personally. So she begins to crowd her love into the daytime hours at Jordan's factory. She presses Paul for little personal intimacies, but he shrinks away from this: "The night is free to you," he says. "In the daytime I want to be by myself. . . . Love-making stifles me in the daytime." But Paul is even more disturbed about another failing: he believes that Clara is unable to "keep his soul steady," that he is simply beyond her, in his creative and intellectual self, and in the breadth and depth of his emotional entanglement—which anticipates a later belief: that men and women must be in balance with each other, as individuals with distinct "life-flows" of their own, before genuine love can flourish. In *Sons and Lovers,* Clara falls short on this count: her "balance" with Paul is scarcely stable, and the growing uneasiness in their affair can be traced, for the most part, to her own inadequacy as an independent being. But even their common bond in passion begins to weaken, under this double burden of "imbalance" and possessive love:

> They did not often reach again the height of that once when the pee-wits called. Gradually, some mechanical effort spoilt their loving, or, when they had splendid moments, they had them separately, and not so satisfactorily. . . .
>
> And afterwards each of them was rather ashamed, and these things caused a distance between the two of them.

This disintegration in love is soon followed by an unexpected but climactic incident. Paul meets Clara's husband one night in a lonely field; Dawes has been waiting for him there and a wild battle follows, in which both opponents are badly damaged. Afterwards, the affair with Clara continues, but only on a mechanical plane: for Dawes has fought with the desperate strength of a man who wants his woman back, and Paul, for all his blind resistance, does not want the woman badly. And so he sheds his dying love in the battle, and a bit later on, he makes his restitution: he finds Dawes in the hospital at Sheffield, befriends him, and gradually brings husband and wife together again.[5] Since Clara really needs her stable, personal, day-time lover, she agrees to the reunion. However that may be, she fails with Paul because of her own shortcomings, for (along with her possessiveness) she lacks the capacity, the breadth of being, to take on the full burden of his troubled soul.

IV

But if both Miriam and Clara defeat themselves, this tells us something important about Mrs. Morel: it is not her interference which destroys her sons, but the strength and peculiar nature of her love. If we switch for a moment to electrical terms, her sons are drawn to her, away from the weaker poles of attraction, because she is the strongest force in the field—and easily the most vital woman in the novel. She is warm and lively, for example, with those she loves, for the early months with her husband were months of passionate fulfill-ment. Though intellectual herself, she was first attracted to Morel by "the dusky, golden softness of his sensuous flame of life"—and this passion for manly, sensual men continues throughout the book. She

---

[5] The strange friendship between Dawes and Morel is one of the first significant male friendships in Lawrence's work. It is based on the attraction-repulsion scheme of all Laurentian loves, and the physical struggle seems to correspond with the famous wrestling scene in *Women in Love*. . . . It should be noted, perhaps, that Dawes is as much the victim of an unjust woman as Walter (or for that matter, Paul) Morel, and this seems to be an important part of his appeal to Paul. . . .

approves, for example, of "the feel of *men* on things," and she takes immediately to the good-looking Mr. Leivers. After her first visit to his farm, she reveals a latent wish to the young lad Paul: "Now *wouldn't* I help that man! . . . *Wouldn't* I see to the fowls and the young stock. And *I'd* learn to milk, and *I'd* talk with him, and *I'd* plan with him. My word, if I were his wife, the farm would be run, I know!"

She also likes the quiet, compact miner, Mr. Barker, who takes good care of his pregnant wife, buys the week's groceries and meats on Friday nights, and keeps a level head. "Barker's little," she tells her husband, "but he's ten times the man you are." And the remark, however vindictive, holds true, for Morel has lost his manhood, and Lawrence gives us ample evidence of this throughout the novel. Unable to live up to his wife's high ideals, afraid of her mind, her will, and above all, her status as "that thing of mystery and fascination, a lady," Morel quarrels with her about money, he takes to drink, begins to mistreat her, and eventually, rather than face the problem in his own home, he retreats from the battle and breaks his own manhood. To be sure, there is a dual responsibility here, since Mrs. Morel has actually driven him to destroy himself. But the fact remains that Lawrence holds his men accountable, in the end, for their own integrity of being, and this will prove an important theme in future novels. The chief irony in *St. Mawr,* for example, is the lack of manhood in the modern world, which drives the heroine to preserve her horse, St. Mawr, as "the last male thing in the universe."

At this point in *Sons and Lovers,* Mrs. Morel turns to her children for fulfillment. And here we run into one of the curious strengths of the book, for the companionship between mother and sons is described, at first, in completely wholesome terms. The destructive potential is there, of course, and Lawrence marks it out as he goes along; but on the whole this is a healthy relationship, and it remains so until the boys come of age. Thus William and Paul are actually kindled to life by their mother's affection; along with the other children, they love to gather about her to discuss the day's events; or they gather berries for Mrs. Morel; they bake bread, blanch walnuts, fetch the father's pay, and exult with her over bargains bought at the marketplace. Indeed, even when Paul falls sick and sleeps with his mother, Lawrence treats the occasion in terms of innocence and health. . . .

Thus, in spite of the general discord in the home, there is also a healthy side to the children's lives, and this helps to account, I think, for the delightful quality of the early scenes between Paul and his mother. On their trip to Nottingham, for instance, Mrs. Morel seems "gay, like a sweetheart," and the two of them feel "the excitement of lovers having an adventure together." But instead of two

lovers, we see nothing more at Jordan's factory than an anxious mother
and a shy, fumbling boy, who botches a "trial" translation for his potential employer. Paul finally gets the job, but there are still more
embarrassing moments ahead: a long wait for a currant tart brings
anguish to the pair; or their zest at a flower shop attracts the stares
of its employees. But incidents like these are scarcely oedipal. There
is the same sheer immersion in simple pleasures, for example, when
Paul and his mother visit the Leivers' farm: on their way across the
fields, they stop to admire a horse, a small truck, and a man silhou-
etted against the sky; Paul calls her attention to a heron floating
above them; he jests at her clumsy manner of mounting stiles; and
later, on the way home, their hearts ache with happiness. The early
scenes between Paul and his mother are almost always like this—
innocent, gay, full of warmth, and marked by lively talk.

But the tenor begins to change once William, the eldest son, dies
in London of pneumonia and erysipelas. The death comes as a terrible
blow to Mrs. Morel, who loved him passionately, and thought of him
almost as "her knight who wore *her* favour in the battle." Now she
loses all interest in life, and remains shut off from the family. But a
few months later, Paul comes down with pneumonia too. "I should
have watched the living, not the dead," she tells herself, and rouses her
strength to save him:

> "I s'll die, mother!" he cried, heaving for breath on the pillow.
> She lifted him up, crying in a small voice:
> "Oh, my son—my son!"
> That brought him to. He realized her. His whole will rose up and
> arrested him. He put his head on her breast, and took ease of her
> love.
> "For some things," said his aunt, "it was a good thing Paul was ill
> that Christmas. I believe it saved his mother."

This scene is an important one, but it is not as oedipal as it seems.
What Lawrence describes here is a legitimate communion, in his eyes.
We have already seen the deeply positive stress which he places upon
sleep with the beloved, and upon the healing qualities of loving touch.
We have also seen the basic health of the mother-son relationship.
Now that health is verified, for when Lawrence writes that Paul
"realized" his mother, he means that Paul has finally reached her,
objectively, in valid, wholesome love. Paul is saved—saved, paradoxically, to be almost destroyed by the oedipal love which follows this
event. For the beauty and richness of the scene is this: Lawrence
has marshalled all the forces of destruction at precisely the same point
at which he has just affirmed, dramatically, all that previous liveliness
and love between Paul and his mother: William, the first son-lover,
has been destroyed; now Paul will take his place in his mother's
heart; he will *become* her second lover, he will in turn be sapped of

his vitality, but at the moment he has just become her most beloved son.

In the years that follow, the relations between Paul and his mother are sometimes rich in satisfaction. He wins prizes for her with his art-work, and she looks upon them as part of her fulfillment. Paul sees it this way too: "All his work was hers." But there are quarrels over his love affairs, and Paul becomes increasingly unhappy. Then, late in the book, he finds "the quick of his trouble": he has loved both Miriam and Clara, but he can belong to neither of them while his mother lives; so long as she holds him, he can never "really love another woman." Thus Lawrence invokes the "split" theory, the pull between mother and sweethearts, to explain his hero's debilitation. But as we have already seen, this theory fails to account for the actual nature of Paul's affairs. We must look elsewhere, then, for the "quick" of his troubles; more specifically, we must look ahead to *Psychoanalysis and the Unconscious* (1921), where Lawrence was finally able to straighten out his views on oedipal love.

In this frontal attack on Freudian psychology, Lawrence decided that the incest-craving is never the normal outcome of the parent-child relationship, but always the result of impressions planted in the child's unconscious mind by an unsatisfied parent. But therefore oedi-pal love is mechanistic, and if mechanistic, then destructive and ab-normal in itself. In one of the late stories, for example, an avaricious mother sends an unspoken whisper through her household—*There must be more money!*—and her young boy destroys himself in his attempts to get it. Now significantly enough, this pattern is already at work in *Sons and Lovers*, though here the whisper runs—*There must be fulfillment!*—as when Paul lies on the sofa, recovering from an early bout with bronchitis:

> He, in his semi-conscious sleep, was vaguely aware of the clatter of the iron on the iron-stand, of the faint thud, thud on the ironing-board. Once roused, he opened his eyes to see his mother standing on the hearthrug with the hot iron near her cheek, listening, as it were, to the heat. Her still face, with the mouth closed tight from suffering and dis-illusion and self-denial, and her nose the smallest bit on one side, and her blue eyes so young, quick, and warm, made his heart contract with love. When she was quiet, so, she looked brave and rich with life, but as if she had been done out of her rights. It hurt the boy keenly, this feeling about her that she had never had her life's fulfilment: and his own incapability to make [it?] up to her hurt him with a sense of im-potence, yet made him patiently dogged inside. It was his childish aim.

Here, then, is the planting of the incest germ, the unwitting im-position of the idea of fulfillment in the young boy's mind. Later on, when Paul becomes the actual agent of his mother's fulfillment, this idea leads inevitably to the incest-craving (through what Law-

rence calls "a logical extension of the existent idea of sex and love,"
Psychoanalysis, p. 24), and from thence to the disintegration of his
essential being. For the proof of this theory, take the constant wran-
gling with his mother; his fury at her old age; the almost violent
quarrel with his father; his own mad restlessness; his obvious "will
to die"; and, after the fight with Dawes, the complete blankness of
his life. He is closer to his mother now than at any stage in the book,
and the only thing which saves him from destruction is her own im-
pending death. For Mrs. Morel falls ill with cancer now, and Paul
cares for her, handling all the details with the doctors, as if he were
the father. He is dazed and isolated from those around him; his grief
stays with him like a mechanical thing which can't be shut off; he
wants his mother to die, but she holds on to life, as always, with her
powerful will; finally, he gives her an overdose of morphia, and this
kills her. He has openly played the lover in these last days, and his
mother, though reduced to a strange, shrivelled-up little girl, is almost
the young wife. But the very desperation of the situation gives it
dignity: this is their special, private, intimate grief over an impossible
dream, and the magnificence of the woman, and the devotional quality
of Paul's love, render the deathbed scenes poignant and innocent.

Paul gives Clara back to her husband after this; he rejects Miriam,
and is himself on the deathward drift, following his mother's spirit.
And it is here, in the final pages, that his debilitation is most clearly
the result, not of any split between mother and sweethearts, but of
his powerful, sterile, obsessive and mechanistic love for his mother.

V

Thus, it is not the "split" theory which gives *Sons and Lovers* its
marvelous power, but the successful dramatization of three destructive
forms of love—oedipal, spiritual, and "unbalanced-possessive." It
seems almost as if Paul were caught, at various times, within the
swirling waters of three terrible whirlpools, each of which drags
him down toward a form of death-in-life; and it is not so much the
violent shifts from one pool to the next which harm him, but the
damage he sustains within each separate pool: and the most deathward
swirl of them all is with his mother.

These three disintegrative loves, when viewed separately, help to
account for the emotional depth of the book. But there is still Paul's
"death" as a son to account for, and his subsequent rebirth as a man,
which Lawrence dimly hints at in the final lines. Paul is alone at night
in the fields outside Nottingham, and wants only to follow his mother
toward the grave—

> But no, he would not give in. Turning sharply, he walked towards the
> city's gold phosphorescence. His fists were shut, his mouth set fast. He

would not take that direction, to the darkness, to follow her. He walked towards the faintly humming, glowing town, quickly.

As Harry Moore points out, Paul's return to life hinges upon the final word, "quickly," which means *livingly* rather than *rapidly:* "The last word in *Sons and Lovers* is an adverb attesting not only to the hero's desire to live but also to his deep ability to do so." [6] And it is this quickness, this vitality, which has enabled Paul to turn away, first from Miriam, then Clara, and now, finally, from his mother. For if Paul has failed in his three loves he has also drawn from them the necessary strength to live. We know, for example, that Paul is a promising young artist, and Lawrence also tells us something significant about his art: "From his mother he drew the life-warmth, the strength to produce, Miriam urged this warmth into intensity like a white light." Now Clara must be considered for she adds to this life-warmth and creative vision the gift of manhood, the "baptism of fire in passion" which will enable Paul "to go on and mature." Indeed, *nothing* can nullify this verification which he and Clara have had together—"it was almost their belief in life":

> As a rule, when he started love-making, the emotion was strong enough to carry with it everything—reason, soul, blood—in a great sweep, like the Trent carries bodily its back-swirls and intertwinings, noiselessly. Gradually, the little criticisms, the little sensations, were lost, thought also went, everything borne along in one flood. He became, not a man with a mind, but a great instinct. . . . It was as if he, and the stars, and the dark herbage, and Clara were licked up in an immense tongue of flame, which tore onwards and upwards. Everything rushed along in living beside him; everything was still, perfect in itself, along with him.

> This wonderful stillness in each thing in itself, while it was being borne along in a very ecstasy of living, seemed the highest point of bliss.

This combination of hurtling along in the sea of life, yet remaining still and perfect in oneself, is the nucleus of Laurentian belief, though we see here only a first rough version of things to come. Nevertheless, at the end of *Sons and Lovers,* we know we have experienced the fact that Paul Morel has achieved a kind of half-realized, or jigsaw success, consisting of mixed elements of life-warmth, creative vision, incipient manhood, and most important of all, a belief (almost) in life itself: and this is the nutritive force which enables him, at the end, to become a man, and to turn quickly toward the glowing city, away from his mother.

[6] *Life and Works*, p. 105. Mr. Moore's observation stands in sharp contrast with Mark Schorer's contention, in "Technique as Discovery," that Paul returns to life "as nothing in his previous history persuades us that he could unfalteringly do." Yet there is nothing "unfaltering" about his final action: it is an act of will, and less a complete rebirth than a choice of direction, or the first stage of a potential resurrection. Nevertheless, it indicates his ascent to manhood for the choice is clear and . . . extremely credible.

The "S" Curve: Persephone to Pluto

by George H. Ford

Autobiographical novels seem to be the easiest kind to write (most of us have one, or parts of one, in a back drawer of a desk), but they are very hard to write well. As the thick volumes of Thomas Wolfe's sprawling novels illustrate, the temptation to throw in almost any experience which occurred in the author's own life, whether or not it contributes to his hero's development, is almost irresistible.

Joyce's solution in his *Portrait* was to exclude ruthlessly any incident or character that did not focus the reader's attention upon Stephen. The style and organization of *Sons and Lovers* is much more casual, much less "engineered" (to use a term of one of Joyce's admirers). Lawrence insisted defensively in a letter that the novel *"is* a unified whole" even though it may be "a bit difficult to grip as a whole, at first." And he added that he hated "the dodge of putting a thick black line round the figures to throw out the composition." Readers, however, are entitled to try imposing such thick black lines, and when they do, it is evident that the structuring of this novel is skillfully devised towards one end, the revelation of "the long and half-secret process" (as Lawrence calls it in his essay on Franklin) of a son's development away from his parents. The organization consists of a sequence of interlocking triangles such as mother-father-son; mother-elder son-girl; mother-son-spiritual girl; mother-son-physical girl. The attention given to William's affair with Gipsy Western may seem, on first reading, carelessly squandered, yet the linking of this triangle to those triangles in which Paul is more immediately connected is crucial, providing the needed preview, the play within the play, of Paul's doomed relationships with Miriam and Clara. And behind the crippled affairs of both sons, and accounting for both, is the crippled marriage of the Morels.

One must beware of the academic fondness for the blackboard diagram, or the easy reduction of Lawrence's subtle complexities into

From "The 'S' Curve: Persephone to Pluto." From Double Measure, A Study of the Novels and Stories of D. H. Lawrence, *by George H. Ford (New York: Holt, Rinehart & Winston, Inc., 1965), pp. 28–44. Copyright © 1965 by George H. Ford. Reprinted by permission of Holt, Rinehart & Winston, Inc.*

the simplified formula, the pap for the undergraduate palates, yet the formula is there.

Zola, in his sometimes fatuously cocky manifesto, *Le roman expéri-mental,* had urged the need for novelists to establish that under such and such conditions of heredity and environment such and such actions and character would inevitably eventuate. It is odd that Law-rence who, like Joyce, was to transform naturalistic techniques beyond recognition, has wittingly or unwittingly followed Zola's prescription in *Sons and Lovers.* The trials and errors of Paul Morel's affairs with Miriam and Clara derived, with the inevitability of cause and effect we expect in naturalistic fiction, from the nature of his parents' marriage.

The married life of the Morels is perhaps the most vivid of Law-rence's many accounts of human conflict. Of their life before marriage we learn little, but there is enough information about their court-ship to predict that such a coupling of opposites will result in strenu-ous tensions. Gertrude Coppard, "a Puritan" and "intellectual" is fascinated by "the dusky, golden softness of this man's sensuous flame of life, that flowed off his flesh like the flame from a candle, not baffled and gripped into incandescence of thought and spirit as her life was." We also learn at the outset, and it is a significant touch, of the miner's proposal at their first meeting, that she should go down with him under the earth. "But tha mun let me ta'e thee down some time, an' tha can see for thysen." Gertrude Morel never did take up the invitation literally, yet the early months of her marriage represent her figurative descent into darkness until she began to fight her way out from it. Later she persuades her children to join her in her ascent and in her repudiation of what her dark mate stood for.

From this matching of opposites derives Paul's crippled love affairs just as from the temptation and fall derived the later events of the Biblical narrative. If we seek such parallels, however, we can in this instance turn not to the Bible, which is usually Lawrence's principal storehouse for analogies, but to a variation of the classical myth of Persephone, to which he makes frequent allusion.

In his version the rape and marriage are the center of interest; the traditional role of the bride's mother, Demeter, is subordinated. It is the tale of a dark man emerging from a cavern in the earth who discovered a fair princess gathering flowers in a field and per-suaded her to be carried off to the underworld where he was a king and where she would reign as his queen. For many months the fair woman was happy in the realms of darkness, but after a time she began to feel she had been taken out of one state of trance only to enter another. And she yearned to return to the land of light where there were white-walled temples, and books, and learned priests. Be-wildered by the dissatisfaction of his wife the dark king fought hard

to prevent her from brooding, but he had to give in and allow her
and their children to return to the land above the underground
darkness.

The narrative is a variant of a familiar classical myth and has
analogies also to the Danish legend of a merman's marriage to a
mortal, a legend on which Matthew Arnold drew for his poem, *The
Foresaken Merman,* with its haunting refrain:

> And alone dwell for ever
> The kings of the sea.

In the classical version, the fair woman was called Persephone (the
name, according to Robert Graves, signifies "she who brings destruction"), and the dark man was Pluto or Hades. In the Lawrentian
version, both in prose and poetry, references to the classical myth
are sometimes made directly. In "The Ladybird," for example, the
dark Count Dionys Psanek reflects upon his affair with Lady Daphne:

> Take her into the underworld. Take her into the dark Hades with
> him, like Francesca and Paolo. And in hell hold her fast, queen of the
> underworld, himself master of the underworld.

In one of the poems, *Bavarian Gentians,* the dark blue of these
"hellish flowers" stimulated the poet to wish that he could witness the
marriage of Persephone and Pluto "as he ravishes her once again/and
pierces her once more." More often the analogy is only indirect, and
the names are remote enough. In the novels the woman is Gertrude
Coppard and the man Walter Morel, or Anna Lensky and Will
Brangwen, or Alvina Houghton and an Italian named Cicio, or Kate
Leslie and Cipriano, a Mexican general, or the virgin Yvette, a clergyman's daughter, and a gipsy who is finally discovered to be named
Joe Boswell. . . . The possible variations of a classic myth, which
Lawrence saw reenacted daily in his own home in Eastwood, provided
him with a seemingly inexhaustible source of inspiration for fiction.

It was suggested earlier that Lawrence's basic narrative consists of
an account of his characters' pursuing a search. The situation in the
Persephone story is often represented as a crucial stage in such a
search, emblematic of the impossibility of a union between opposites
and the consequent loneliness of strangers sharing a bed for a lifetime, strangers who remain strangers. . . .

How did Lawrence regard the conflict between Walter and Gertrude Morel? And how did he expect us, as readers, to regard them?
Was the Persephone figure "right" in her repudiation of her dark
mate, or is the subject of right and wrong inappropriate in this
instance? So phrased, such questions sound schoolmistressly simple,
yet to attempt to answer them can lead into some of the principal
problems that confront us in discussing Lawrence's writings.

One such problem is that of heroes and villains. The role of the hero in literature has become almost obsessively topical in recent literary criticism, and it is therefore of interest to have George Orwell's report on what surprised him when he first read Lawrence's fiction.

When I first read D. H. Lawrence's novels, at the age of about twenty, I was puzzled by the fact that there did not seem to be any classification of the characters into "good" and "bad." Lawrence seemed to sympathise with all of them about equally and this was so unusual as to give me the feeling of having lost my bearings. Today no one would think of looking for heroes and villains in a serious novel.

Orwell's statement may appear to be mere nonsense. As a man, Lawrence was as dogmatic and intensely opinionated as his Victorian predecessor, John Ruskin, and his opinions took in as many subjects as Ruskin had embraced. How could such a man create a world without villains and heroes?

When he portrays the managing-engineer, Uncle Tom Brangwen, in *The Rainbow,* it is evident that the writer's loathing of industrialism has produced a hatefully villainous figure. Descriptions such as the following seethe with dislike:

The fine beauty of his skin and his complexion, some almost waxen quality, hid the strange, repellent grossness of him, the slight sense of putrescence, the commonness which revealed itself in his rather fat thighs and loins.

Moreover, if Uncle Tom Brangwen is a villain it is also evident that other characters have been distinctly cast in heroic mold: Don Ramón in *The Plumed Serpent,* for example, or other leaders who bear a resemblance to Lawrence himself. It would be remarkable if the twentieth-century descendent of Carlyle, the author of *Heroes and Hero-Worship,* had written novels in which heroes have been eclipsed.

Yet despite all the qualifying clauses that my objections suggest, Orwell's observation is ultimately a sound one. It provides a helpful corrective against the kind of reader who salivates his way through Lawrence's books as if they were stories of infallible heroes righteously disposing of wicked industrialists or other categories of the unredeemed. Carlyle and Ruskin wrote tracts and essays, and made very few excursions into fiction; Lawrence wrote fiction and occasionally tried his hand at tracts and essays. Especially in his later work, the tracts and essays ("pollyanalytics" he called them) do get into the fiction inevitably, for as was suggested earlier Lawrence is certainly not the fastidious aesthetic novelist. A mixture of discourse and image is usually present, and from novels such as *Women in Love* we can distill the discourse to our satisfaction and conclude that we then have the book adequately bottled and labeled. But the distillation process has captured a vapor; the novel that Lawrence wrote is not to be thus confined. For the characteristic rhythm in his fiction is double: thesis thrusting against antithesis, lion against unicorn, darkness against light. Gertrude Morel, that is, is not a good force struggling against a bad force, but simply one kind of force, and her husband another kind. It is this sort of balancing that accounts for Orwell's impression of there being no villains or heroes in the novels. . . .

When Walter Morel gets up at dawn to prepare his own breakfast, Lawrence observes that "he preferred to keep the blinds down and the candle lit even when it was daylight." What is meant by associating "darkness" with the father in *Sons and Lovers* and "light" with the mother ought to be generally clear to most readers of Lawrence. The terms are intended to signify contrasting kinds of experience (unconscious or conscious); contrasting ways of acquiring knowledge (through the senses or through reason); contrasting concepts of social structure (static and traditional as in a primitive tribe or dynamic and progressive as in an expanding urban society). . . .

The world of light involves conscious awareness in place of instinctive knowledge. When Ursula Brangwen receives a proposal of marriage from Anthony Schofield, she is attracted physically to the young farmer, but recognizes sadly that his inner world is altogether different from her own:

> He was an animal that knows it is subdued. Her heart flamed with sensation of him, of the fascinating thing he offered her, and with sorrow, and with an inconsolable sense of loneliness. Her soul was an infant crying in the night. He had no soul. Oh, and why had she?

In *The White Peacock* the same distinction is made more playfully by Lettie when she teases the farmer, George Saxton: "You are blind; you are only half born; you are gross with good living and heavy sleeping. . . . Sunset is nothing to you—it merely happens anywhere."

Furthermore, light may be associated with change of social status. Among the Brangwen women, as with Mrs. Morel, there is a desire not only for intellectual development but for an advancement of their sons from one social class to another. Their sense of time is what the sociologists call "future-oriented" whereas their husbands enjoy instead a relatively "future-ignoring present."

A coal miner may be proud of his work, but as Richard Hoggart emphasizes in his study of working-class attitudes, *The Uses of Literacy,* he has no illusions about the possibility of changing his status and hence very little sense of competitiveness. Light is usually a middle-class attribute, Persephone a middle-class goddess. Finally, light is more often associated with women than with men, but the division is not always so neat. The clergyman, emancipated from the soil and mine, belongs to the world of light as does the industrialist Gerald Crich in *Women in Love*. Most complex of all are men such as Rupert Birkin in the same novel who is related to light but has some intellectual commitment to the values of darkness which at times he seems to be advocating. As stated in the *Last Poems* volume:

> Hell is the home of souls lost in darkness,
> even as heaven is the home of souls lost in light.

And the poet adds: "there are souls that are at home in both homes." . . .

These preliminaries serve to clear the ground for the question previously raised: how did Lawrence regard the elder Morels? Is *Sons and Lovers* an exposé, like Butler's *The Way of All Flesh* or Aldington's *Death of a Hero*, of a hateful paternal tyranny? In later life Lawrence himself asserted ruefully that he had loaded his dice in *Sons and Lovers* because his portrait of Walter Morel, he then believed, had been harsh and unkind. And from additional evidence concerning his early feelings towards his own father, the model for Walter Morel, we should be led to expect a savage cartoon. "I have to hate him for Mother's sake," the young Bert Lawrence told May Chambers, and the intensity of his hatred astonished her. . . .

In October, 1910, he assured one correspondent that he had "never had but one parent," and in the following February, three months after the death of his mother, he exclaimed in a letter that he wished his father were in Hell, and added: "I shivered with horror when he touched me." What remains remarkable is that in rewriting *Sons and Lovers* during the following year, Lawrence was able so largely to master his private hatreds and to create, in Walter Morel, not only a vivid portrait (one of the most vividly *presented* characters in all his fiction) but also a portrait of a man with whom the reader can sympathize. "Paul hated his father so," says the novelist, and under the unflinching spotlight we see the father as we might expect to see him:

> The collier's small, mean head . . . lay on the bare arms, and the face, dirty and inflamed, with a fleshy nose . . . was turned sideways, asleep with beer and weariness and nasty temper.

The spotlight focuses not only upon Walter Morel's physical grossness but upon his ultimate ineffectuality, his blustering threats to leave home and his ignominious return. Yet the portrait remains a portrait and not a cartoon because of the man's vitality and because of his isolation. The picture of his solitary breakfast is unforgettable, concluding as it does with these two sentences:

> He loved the early morning, and the walk across the fields. So he ap-

peared at the pit-top, often with a stalk from the hedge between his
teeth, which he chewed all day to keep his mouth moist, down the
mine, feeling quite as happy as when he was in the field.

That wonderful touch of the hedge stalk, which endows the collier
with the dimensions of an earth spirit, is the kind of detail that can-
cels out scenes in which he seems merely "despicable." Most of all,
however, to achieve balance, Lawrence shows Morel as a man to
be pitied. He becomes, in his own home, an "outsider" as Lawrence
calls him (an epithet which gained notoriety through Colin Wilson,
author of *The Outsider,* and also, oddly enough, a severe critic of
Lawrence). Morel's isolation is emphasized by his blackness as he
roars in out of the dark night and by his dialect. Like a first-gen-
eration immigrant in the United States, his every sentence puts a
gulf between himself and his children, who speak a different language.[1] His total isolation, at the end, when his wife is dying, is
pictured in scenes that impressed Ada Lawrence as "too deep for
tears." One need not have been a member of the Lawrence family
to endorse her tribute.

The balancing achieved in the presentation of Mrs. Morel is of
a different order. As we close the book, with the death scenes in
mind, our impression may be that the whole novel has been in the
tender elegiac vein of the poems Lawrence wrote after his own
mother died. Most readers would agree with Walter Allen when he
notes that the novelist is distinctly on the side of the mother. *Sons
and Lovers* was written by Persephone's son, yet its portrait of the
Persephone figure is much more inclusive than elegiac conventions
allow. The spotlight is as unflinchingly turned on Mrs. Morel as
it was upon her husband, only in her case, it is the destructiveness
of her love in her relationship with others that is exposed.

In recent years, in fact, it has been my experience to encounter
readers who argue that Mrs. Morel is a villainous woman, totally
incapable of arousing sympathy on the part of any observant reader.
She was responsible, they point out, for driving her husband to drink
and isolation, for driving one son to death and another to the point
of death. The indictment leaves out of account the tenderness of
tone—that indefinable quality in drama or fiction—with which
Lawrence surrounds his portrait, and with which, in the film version,

---

[1] In some of the love scenes Paul uses dialect as it is used by Mellors in *Lady
Chatterley's Lover* as a kind of lovers' shorthand, a shift into the language of tenderness. The comic possibilities of dialect are also evident, although one suspects
Lawrence eliminated some of the broader touches, on Garnett's advice, when he
revised *Sons and Lovers.* In his play, *A Collier's Friday Night,* when the miner's
daughter refuses to hang up the father's wet pit-trousers to dry, he comments: "I
wonder how er'd like to clep 'er arse into wet breeches." In the novel this is toned
down to "Should thee like to clap thysen into britches as cowd as a tub o' water?"

a distinguished and beautiful actress, Wendy Hiller, was able to endow the role. And yet the indictment is accurate enough. The facts are all there in the novel, but it takes a shift of attitudes, in a later generation, to force the inferences to be made. . . .

That Lawrence's portrait of the dedicated and energetic Mrs. Morel could be taken by earlier readers (including Jessie Chambers) as an idealization of motherhood and by some later readers as an exposé of motherhood is, in itself, testimony to the balancing which I am suggesting is characteristic of his best work. In 1913 Lawrence wrote to Garnett:

> I had a devil of a time getting a bit weaned from my mother, at the age of 22. She suffered, and I suffered, and it seemed all for nothing, just waste cruelty. It's funny. I suppose it's the final breaking away to independence.

Here is a main subject of *Sons and Lovers*, a subject with kinetic potential. That the novel has affected attitudes of readers is probable, but if we are to classify Lawrence as a kinetic writer (as he is usually classified in contrast to Joyce) it should be with the reservation suggested here.

Butler's *The Way of All Flesh*, a typical publication of the post-Victorian era, is a frontal attack on what seemed to its author to be a tyrannical institution, the family. Butler, like Harriet Beecher Stowe in *Uncle Tom's Cabin*, did his work well but not well enough to keep his novel truly fresh.

Sons and Lovers is not an attack against fathers, or mothers, or families. It is a record of a family and of the pathos of its complex interrelationships. . . .

One reason that Lawrence was able to achieve variety in presenting his basic drama of the dark man and fair woman was that his own attitude towards the protagonists gradually changed.

When Mrs. Lawrence was dying of cancer in 1910, she finally recognized the futility of her long struggle against her husband. As Lawrence says in his essay, "Women Are So Cocksure":

> And at fifty, when the best part of life was gone, she realized it. And then what would she not have given to have her life again, her young children, her tipsy husband, and a proper natural insouciance, to get the best out of it all. When woman tries to be too much mistress of fate, particularly of other people's fates, what a tragedy!

The significance of Mrs. Lawrence's admission does not seem to have made its full impact on her son in 1910; his own realization of it came later. I suspect that the incident accounts for a curious shift of tone that occurs in *The Lost Girl*. The first part of this novel, written early in 1913, seems to have been infected by his reading of Arnold Bennett, especially the mockingly jocular tone Bennett used to describe life in a small Midlands town. The opening pages of *The Lost Girl* sustain this jocular tone effectively, but in one early scene there is a sudden shift into a different key as Lawrence recalls what his mother had said on her deathbed. When the fifty-two-year-old Miss Frost breaks down into tears before Alvina, her crying is described as "the terrible crying of a woman with a loving heart, whose heart has never been able to relax."

> The terrible sound of "Never now, never now—it is too late," which seemed to ring in the curious, indrawn cries of the elder woman, filled the girl with a deep wisdom. She knew the same would ring in her mother's dying cry. Married or unmarried, it was the same—the same anguish, realised in all its pain after the age of fifty—the loss in never having been able to relax, to submit.

This passage, written after *Sons and Lovers* had been completed, suggests that Lawrence was moving away from the stage of hatred for his father to a stage of understanding his father. In the autumn of 1914 he grew a beard.

The main line of Lawrence's development from this time forward follows what psychoanalysts sometimes describe as an "S" curve. Many of us, in our early years, exhibit a passionate preference for one parent, and his or her standards, and then gradually shift allegiance later. The boy who dotes upon his mother and despises his father can become a man who realizes that his mother's standards were inadequate or stultifying and that what his father had stood for is what the son now recognizes as valid.

The "S" curve may be detected in Mark Twain's jest about reaching the age of twenty-one and being astonished to realize how much his father had learned in the preceding five years. Lawrence had to be much older than twenty-one before the discovery grew upon him.

In 1926 when he was forty-one years old, he told Barbara Weekley that he had "formerly hated his drunken father, but at this time had swung his sympathy towards him, away from his mother." And in a late autobiographical sketch, as yet unpublished, he is even more explicit about his switch of allegiance:

> My mother fought with deadly hostility against my father, all her life. He was not hostile, till provoked, then he too was a devil. But my mother began it. She seemed to begrudge his very existence. She begrudged him and hated her own love for him, she fought against his natural charm, vindictively. And by the time she died, at the age of fifty-five, she neither loved nor hated him any more. She had got over her feeling for him, and was "Free." So she died of cancer. Her feeling for us, also was divided. We were her own, therefore she loved us. But we were his, so she despised us a little. I was the most delicate. . . . She loved me tenderly. . . . But now, in the after years, I realize that she had decided I was going to die, and that was a great deal to her.

This realization may have been crystallized in 1924 when Lawrence's father died. The event, which Freudians in particular regard as one of the principal turning points in a man's life, was rarely mentioned by Lawrence. Like James Joyce, whose love for his improvident father was the principal love of his life (according to his brother's testimony), Lawrence had seemingly broken all ties with the man himself. Joyce treated his father to an occasional postcard; Lawrence, whose father could scarcely read, may not have managed even that token of contact. What mattered to both writers was not the actual aging parent but what each had stood for in earlier years. To this image both novelists returned in their writings.

If the "S" curve signifies the main line of Lawrence's development, it should be noted that the line cannot be represented as an unbroken progress. There are many points of turning back. Yet in his characteristic fictional mode of balancing one set of forces against an opposite set of forces, we can readily detect a change of emphasis between his early and late writings. A change of values, implied or explicitly stated, tips the balance from Persephone's side to Pluto's.

Sons, Lovers, and Mothers

by Alfred Kazin

Sons and Lovers was published fifty years ago. In these fifty years
how many autobiographical novels have been written by young men
about the mothers they loved too well, about their difficulties in "ad-
justing" to other women, and about themselves as the sensitive writers-
to-be who liberated themselves just in time in order to write their
first novel? Such autobiographical novels—psychological devices they
usually are, written in order to demonstrate freedom from the all-
too-beloved mother—are one of the great symbols of our time. They
are rooted in the modern emancipation of women. Lawrence himself,
after a return visit in the 1920's to his native Nottinghamshire, la-
mented that the "wildness" of his father's generation was gone, that
the dutiful sons in his own generation now made "good" husbands.
Even working-class mothers in England, in the last of the Victorian
age, had aimed at a "higher" standard of culture, and despising their
husbands and concentrating on their sons, they had made these sons
images of themselves. These mothers had sought a new dignity and
even a potential freedom for themselves as women, but holding their
sons too close, they robbed them of their necessary "wildness" and
masculine force. So the sons grew up in bondage to their mothers,
and the more ambitious culturally these sons were—Frank O'Connor
says that *Sons and Lovers* is the work of "one of the New Men who
are largely a creation of the Education Act of 1870"—the more likely
they were to try for their emancipation by writing a novel. The cultural aspiration that explains their plight was expected to turn them
into novelists.

Sons and Lovers (which is not a first novel) seems easy to imitate.
One reason, apart from the relationships involved, is the very directness and surface conventionality of its technique. James Joyce's *A Portrait of the Artist As a Young Man,* published only three years after
Sons and Lovers, takes us immediately into the "new" novel of the
twentieth century. It opens on a bewildering series of images faithful

*"Sons, Lovers, and Mothers." Introduction by Alfred Kazin to the Modern Library
Edition of* Sons and Lovers *(New York: Random House, Inc., 1962), pp. vii–xix.
Copyright 1962 by Alfred Kazin. Reprinted by permission of the author.*

to the unconsciousness of childhood. Proust, who brought out the
first volume of his great novel, *A la recherche du temps perdu*, in the
same year that Lawrence published *Sons and Lovers*, imposed so
highly stylized a unity of mood on the "Ouverture" to *Du côté de
chez Swann*, that these impressions of childhood read as if they had
been reconstructed to make a dream. But *Sons and Lovers* opens as
a nineteenth-century novel with a matter-of-fact description of the setting—the mine, the landscape of "Bestwood," the neighboring streets
and houses. This opening could have been written by Arnold Bennett,
or any other of the excellent "realists" of the period whose work does
not summon up, fifty years later, the ecstasy of imagination that
Lawrence's work, along with that of Joyce and Proust, does provide
to us. Lawrence is writing close to the actual facts. In his old-fashioned
way he is even writing *about* the actual facts. No wonder that a
young novelist with nothing but *his* own experiences to start him
off may feel that Lawrence's example represents the triumph of experience. Literature has no rites in *Sons and Lovers;* everything follows as if from memory alone. When the struggle begins that makes
the novel—the universal modern story of a "refined" and discontented
woman who pours out on her sons love she refuses the husband too
"common" for her—the equally universal young novelist to whom
all this has happened, the novelist who in our times is likely to have
been all too mothered and fatherless, cannot help saying to himself—
"Why can't I write this good a novel out of myself? Haven't I suffered
as much as D. H. Lawrence and am I not just as sensitive? And isn't
this a highly selective age in which 'sensitive' writers count?"

But the most striking thing about Lawrence—as it is about Paul
Morel in this novel—is his sense of his own authority. Though he
was certainly not saved from atrocious suffering in relation to his
mother, Lawrence's "sensitivity" was in the main concerned with
reaching the highest and widest possible consciousness of everything—
"nature," family, society, books—that came within his experience
as a human being. His sense of his own powers, of himself as a
"medium" through which the real life in things could be discovered
for other people, was so strong that his personal vividness stayed with
his earliest friends as a reminder of the best hopes of their youth; it
was instantly recognized by literary people in London when they
read his work. You can easily dislike Lawrence for this air of authority,
just as many people dislike him for the influence that he exerted
during his lifetime and that has grown steadily since his death in
1930. There is already an unmistakeable priggish conceit about Paul
Morel in this novel. Here is a miner's son who is asked by his mother
if his is a "divine discontent" and replies in this style: "Yes. I don't
care about its divinity. But damn your happiness! So long as life's
full, it doesn't matter whether it's happy or not. I'm afraid your

happiness would bore me." But even this contains Lawrence's sense
of his own authority. He saw his talent as a sacred possession—he
was almost too proud to think of his career as a *literary* one. This
sense of having a power that makes for righteousness—this was so
strong in Lawrence, and so intimately associated with his mother's influence, that the struggle he describes in *Sons and Lovers,* the struggle
to love another woman as he had loved his mother, must be seen as
the connection he made between his magic "demon," his gift, and his
relationship to his mother.

Freud once wrote that he who is a favorite of the mother becomes
a "conqueror." This was certainly Freud's own feeling about himself.
The discoverer of the Oedipus complex never doubted that the attachment which, abnormally protracted, makes a son feel that loving any
woman but his mother is a "desecration," nevertheless, in its early
prime features, gives a particular kind of strength to the son. It is
a spiritual strength, not the masculine "wildness" that Lawrence was
to miss in contemporary life. Lawrence's own feeling that he was certainly somebody, the pride that was to sustain him with horribly
damaged lungs through so many years of tuberculosis until his death
at forty-five; the pride that carried him so far from a miner's cottage;
the pride that enabled him, a penniless schoolteacher, to run off with
a German baroness married to his old teacher and to make her give
up her three children; the pride that thirty years after his death still
makes him so vivid to us as we read—this pride had not its origin
but its *setting,* in the fierce love of Mrs. Arthur Lawrence for "Bert,"
of Mrs. Morel for her Paul.

Lawrence, who was so full of his own gift, so fully engaged in
working it out that he would not acknowledge his gifted contemporaries, certainly did feel that the "essential soul" of him as he would
have said, his special demon, his particular gift of vision, his particular claim on immortality, was bound up with his mother. Not
"love" in the psychological sense of conscious consideration, but love
in the mythological sense of a sacred connection, was what Lawrence
associated with his mother and Paul with Mrs. Morel. Lawrence's
power over others is directly traceable to his own sense of the sacred-
ness still possible to life, arising from the powers hidden in ordinary
human relationships. The influence he had—if only temporarily—
even on a rationalist like Bertrand Russell reminds one of the hold
he kept on socialist working-class people he had grown up with and
who certainly did not share Lawrence's exalted individualism. Lawrence's "authority" which made him seem unbearably full of himself
to those who disliked him, was certainly of a very singular kind. He
had an implicit confidence in his views on many questions—on politics as on sex and love; he was able to pontificate in later life about
the Etruscans, of whom he knew nothing, as well as to talk dangerous

nonsense about "knowing through the blood" and the leader principle. Yet it is Lawrence's struggle to retain all the moral authority that he identified with his mother's love that explains the intensity of *Sons and Lovers,* as it does the particular intensity of Lawrence's style in this book, which he later criticized as too violent. Yet behind this style lies Lawrence's lifelong belief in what he called "quickness," his need to see the "shimmer," the life force in everything, as opposed to the "dead crust" of its external form. Destiny for Lawrence meant his privileged and constant sense of the holiness implicit in this recognition of the life force. Destiny also meant his recognition, as a delicate boy who had already seen his older brother Ernest (the "William" of *Sons and Lovers*) sicken and die of the struggle to attach himself to another woman, that his survival was somehow bound up with fidelity to his mother. Lawrence had absolute faith in his gift, but it was bound up with his physical existence, which was always on trial. He felt that it was in his mother's hands. The gift of life, so particularly precious to him after his near-fatal pneumonia at seventeen (after his brother died), could be easily lost.

With so much at stake, Lawrence put into ultimate terms, life or death, the struggle between Paul Morel's need to hold onto his mother and his desire to love Miriam Leivers as well. The struggle in *Sons and Lovers* is not between love of the mother and love of a young woman; it is the hero's struggle to *keep* the mother as his special strength, never to lose her, not to offend or even to vex her by showing too much partiality to other women. This is why the original of "Miriam Leivers," Jessie Chambers, says in her touching memoir (*D. H. Lawrence: A Personal Record:* by "E. T.") that she had to break with Lawrence after she had seen the final draft of the book, that "the shock of *Sons and Lovers* gave the death-blow to our friendship," for in that book "Lawrence handed his mother the laurels of victory."

That is indeed what Lawrence did; it would not have occurred to him to do anything else. And Jessie Chambers also honestly felt that she minded this for Lawrence's sake, not her own, since by this time there was no longer any question of marriage between them. Jessie, who certainly loved Lawrence for his genius even after she had relinquished all personal claim on him, had launched Lawrence's career by sending out his poems. When Lawrence, after his mother's death, wrote a first draft of *Sons and Lovers,* he was still unable to work out his situation in a novel. Jessie encouraged him to drop this unsatisfactory version of the later novel and to portray the emotional struggle directly. At his request, she even wrote out narrative sections which Lawrence revised and incorporated into his novel. (Lawrence often had women write out passages for his novels when he wanted to know how a woman would react to a particular situation;

Frieda Lawrence was to contribute to his characterization of Mrs. Morel.) Lawrence sent Jessie parts of the manuscript for her comments and further notes. After so much help and even collaboration, Jessie felt betrayed by the book. Lawrence had failed to show, she said, how important a role the girl had played in the development of the young man as an artist. "It was his old inability to face his problem squarely. His mother had to be supreme, and for the sake of that supremacy every disloyalty was permissible."

Lawrence is quoted in Harry T. Moore's biography, *The Intelligent Heart,* as saying of Miriam-Jessie, she "encouraged my demon. But alas, it was me, not he, whom she loved. So for her too it was a catastrophe. My demon is not easily loved: whereas the ordinary me is. So poor Miriam was let down." Lawrence's tone is exalted, but he certainly justified himself in *Sons and Lovers* as a novelist, not as a "son." That is the only consideration now. Jessie Chambers herself became an embittered woman. She tried to find her salvation in politics, where the fierce hopes of her generation before 1914 for a new England were certainly not fulfilled. But Lawrence, taking the new draft of *Sons and Lovers* with him to finish in Germany after he had run off with Frieda, was able, if not to "liberate" himself from his mother in his novel, to write a great novel out of his earliest life and struggles.

That is the triumph Jessie Chambers would not acknowledge in *Sons and Lovers,* that she could not see—the Lawrence "unable to face his problem squarely" made a great novel out of the "problem," out of his mother, father, brother, the miners, the village, the youthful sweetheart. Whatever Jessie may have thought from being too close to Lawrence himself, whatever Lawrence may have said about his personal struggles during the six-week frenzy in which he launched the new draft, Lawrence felt his "problem" not as something to be solved, but as a subject to be represented. All these early experiences weighed on him with a pressure that he was able to communicate— later he called it "that hard violent style full of sensation and presentation." Jessie Chambers herself described Lawrence's accomplishment when she said, speaking of the new draft of *Sons and Lovers* that she drove Lawrence to write, "It was his power to transmute the common experiences into significance that I always felt to be Lawrence's greatest gift. He did not distinguish between small and great happenings. The common round was full of mystery, awaiting interpretation. Born and bred of working people, he had the rare gift of seeing them from within, and revealing them on their own plane."

Lawrence's particular gift was this ability to represent as valuable anything that came his way. He had the essential religious attribute of *valuing* life, of seeing the most trivial things as a kind of consecration. In part, at least, one can trace this to the poverty, austerity

and simplicity of his upbringing. Jessie Chambers once watched Lawrence and his father gathering watercress for tea. "Words cannot convey Lawrence's brimming delight in all these simple things." Delight
in simple things is one of the recurring features of the working-class
existence described in *Sons and Lovers*. We can understand better the
special value that Lawrence identified with his mother's laboriousness
and self-denial in the scene where Mrs. Morel, wickedly extravagant,
comes home clutching the pot that cost her fivepence and the bunch
of pansies and daisies that cost her fourpence. The rapture of the com-
monest enjoyments and simplest possessions is represented in the
mother and father as well as in the young artist Paul, the future
D. H. Lawrence. This autobiographical novel rooted in the writer's
early struggles is charged with feeling for his class, his region, his people. Lawrence was not a workingman himself, despite the brief experience in the surgical appliances factory that in the novel becomes Paul
Morel's continued job. Chekhov said that the working-class writer pur-
chases with his youth that which a more genteel writer is born with.
But Lawrence gained everything, as a writer, from being brought up
in the working class, and lost nothing by it. In *Sons and Lovers* he
portrays the miners without idealizing them, as a socialist would; he
relishes their human qualities (perhaps even a little jealously) and
works them up as a subject for his art. He does not identify himself
with them; his mother, too, we can be sure from the portrait of Mrs.
Morel, tended to be somewhat aloof among the miners' wives. But
Lawrence knows *as a writer* that he is related to working people, that
he is bound up with them in the same order of physical and intimate
existence, that it is workers' lives he has always looked on. Some of
the most affecting passages in this novel are based on the force and
directness of working-class speech. " 'E's niver gone, child?" Morel
says to his son when William dies. Paul answers in "educated" and
even prissy English, but the voice of the mines, the fields and the
kitchens is rendered straight and unashamed. Lawrence, who knew
how much he had lost as a man by siding with his mother in the conflict, describes the miner Morel getting his own breakfast, sitting
"down to an hour of joy," with an irresistible appreciation of the
physical and human picture involved: "He toasted his bacon on
a fork and caught the drops of fat on his bread; then he put the
rasher on his thick slice of bread, and cut off chunks with a clasp-
knife, poured his tea into his saucer, and was happy."

The writer alone in Lawrence redeemed the weaknesses of being
too much of his mother's son. We see the common round of life among
the miners' families very much as the young Lawrence must have
seen it, with the same peculiar directness. His mental world was
startlingly without superfluities and wasted motions. What he wrote,
he wrote. The striking sense of authority, of inner conviction, that he

associated with his mother's love gave him a cutting briskness with things he disapproved. But this same immediacy of response, when it touched what he loved, could reach the greatest emotional depths. The description of William Morel's coffin being carried into the house is a particular example of this. "The coffin swayed, the men began to mount the three steps with their load. Annie's candle flickered, and she whimpered as the first men appeared, and the limbs and bowed heads of six men struggled to climb into the room, bearing the coffin that rode like sorrow on their living flesh." Lawrence's power to move the reader lies in this ability to summon up all the physical attributes associated with an object; he puts you into direct contact with all its properties *as* an object. Rarely has the realistic novelist's need to *present,* to present vividly, continually, and at the highest pitch of pictorial concentration—the gift which has made the novel the supreme literary form of modern times—rarely has this reached such intense clarity of representation as it does in *Sons and Lovers.* There are passages in *Sons and Lovers,* as in Tolstoy, that make you realize what a loss to directness of vision our increasing self-consciousness in literature represents. Lawrence is still face to face with life, and he can describe the smallest things with the most attentive love and respect.

Lawrence does not describe, he would not attempt to describe, the object as in *itself* it really is. The effect of his prose is always to heighten our consciousness of something, to relate it to ourselves. He is a romantic—and in this book is concerned with the most romantic possible subject for a novelist, the growth of the writer's own consciousness. Yet he succeeded as a novelist, he succeeded brilliantly, because he was convinced that the novel is the great literary form, for no other could reproduce so much of the actual motion or "shimmer" of life, especially as expressed in the relationships between people. Since for Lawrence the great subject of literature was not the writer's own consciousness but consciousness between people, the living felt relationship between them, it was his very concern to represent the "shimmer" of life, the "wholeness"—these could have been mere romantic slogans—that made possible his brilliance as a novelist. He was to say, in a remarkable essay called "Why The Novel Matters," that "Only in the novel are *all* things given full play, or at least, they may be given full play, when we realize that life itself, and not inert safety, is the reason for living. For out of the full play of all things emerges the only thing that is anything, the wholeness of a man, the wholeness of a woman, man alive, and live woman." It was relationship that was sacred to him, as it was the relationship with his mother, her continuing presence in his mind and life, that gave him that sense of authority on which all his power rested. And as a novelist in *Sons and Lovers* he was able to rise above every conventional pitfall in an autobiographical novel by centering his whole vision on character as the focus of a relationship, not as an absolute.

After *Sons and Lovers,* which was his attempt to close up the past, Lawrence was to move on to novels like *The Rainbow* (1915) and *Women In Love* (1920), where the "non-human in humanity" was to be more important to him than "the old-fashioned human element." The First World War was to make impossible for Lawrence his belief in the old "stable ego" of character. Relationships, as the continuing interest of life, became in these more "problematical," less "conventional" novels, a version of man's general relationship, as an unknown to himself, to his unexplained universe. But the emphasis on growth and change in *Sons and Lovers,* the great book that closes Lawrence's first period, is from the known to the unknown; as Frank O'Connor has said, the book begins as a nineteenth-century novel and turns into a twentieth-century one.[1] Where autobiographical novels with a "sensitive" artist or novelist as hero tend to emphasize the hero's growth to self-knowledge, the history of his "development," the striking thing about *Sons and Lovers,* and an instance of the creative mind behind it, is that it does not hand the "laurels of victory" to the hero. It does not allow him any self-sufficient victory over his circumstances. With the greatest possible vividness it shows Paul Morel engulfed in relationships—with the mother he loves all too sufficiently, with the "spiritual" Miriam and Clara, neither of whom he can love whole-heartedly—relationships that are difficult and painful, and that Lawrence leaves arrested in their pain and conflict. When Jessie Chambers said of the first draft of *Sons and Lovers* that "Lawrence had carried the situation to the point of deadlock and had stopped there," she may have been right enough about it as an aborted novel. But Lawrence's primary interest and concern as a novelist, his sense of the continuing *flow* of relationship between people, no matter how unclear and painful, no matter how far away it was from the "solution" that the people themselves may have longed for, is what makes this whole last section of the novel so telling.

But of course it is the opening half of *Sons and Lovers* that makes the book great. The struggle between husband and wife is described with a direct, unflinching power. Lawrence does not try to bring anything to a psychological conclusion. The marriage is a struggle, a continuing friction, a relationship where the wife's old desire for her husband can still flash up through her resentment of his "lowness." That is why everything in the "common round" can be described with such tenderness, for the relationship of husband and wife sweeps into its unconscious passion everything that the young Lawrence loved, and was attached to. Living in a mining village on

[1] [Frank O'Connor's discussion of *Sons and Lovers* appears on pp. 101–5 of this volume.]

the edge of old Sherwood Forest, always close to the country, Lawrence was as intimate with nature as any country poet could have
been, but he was lucky to see rural England and the industrial Midlands in relation to each other; the country soothed his senses, but
a job all day long in a Nottingham factory making out orders for
surgical appliances did not encourage nature worship. "On the fallow
land the young wheat shone silkily. Minton pit waved its plumes
of white steam, coughed, and rattled hoarsely." Lawrence is a great
novelist *of* landscape, for he is concerned with the relationships of
people living on farms, or walking out into the country after the
week's work in the city. He does not romanticize nature, he describes it in its minute vibrations. In *Sons and Lovers* the emotional
effect of the "lyrical" passages depends on Lawrence's extraordinary
ability to convey movement and meaning even in nonhuman things.
But in this book nature never provides evasion of human conflict and
is not even a projection of human feelings; it is the physical world
that Lawrence grew up in, and includes the pit down which a miner
must go every day. Paul in convalescence, sitting up in bed, would
"see the fluffy horses feeding at the troughs in the field, scattering
their hay on the trodden yellow snow; watch the miners troop home—
small, black figures trailing slowly in gangs across the white field."

This miniature, exquisite as a Japanese watercolor, is typical of
the book—in *Sons and Lovers* the country lives and seethes, but it
has no mystical value. It is the landscape of Nottinghamshire and
Derbyshire, and in the book is still what it was to Lawrence growing
up in it, an oasis of refreshment in an industrial world. The countryside arouses young lovers to their buried feelings and it supplies images for the "quickness," the vital current of relationship, that Lawrence valued most in life. It is never sacred in itself. When you consider that this novel came out in 1913, at the height of the "Georgian"
period, when so many young poets of Lawrence's generation were
mooning over nature, it is striking that *his* chief interest is always
the irreducible ambiguity of human relationships. Lawrence's language, in certain key scenes, certainly recalls the emotional inflation
of fiction in the "romantic" heyday preceding World War I. But the
style is actually exalted rather than literary. There is an unmistakably
scriptural quality to Lawrence's communication of extreme human
feeling. Mr. Morel secretly cuts young William's hair, and Mrs. Morel
feels that "this act of masculine clumsiness was the spear through
the side of her love." The Lawrences were Congregationalist, like
American Puritans. They felt close to the Lord. The strong sense of
himself that Lawrence was always to have, the conviction that what
he felt was always terribly important just in the way he felt it, is im-
parted to Mrs. Morel herself in the great scene in which the insulted
husband, dizzy with drink, locks her out of the house. The description

of Mrs. Morel's feelings is charged with a kind of frenzy of concern for her; the language sweeps from pole to pole of feeling. Mrs. Morel is pregnant, and her sense of her moral aloneness at this moment is overwhelming. "Mrs. Morel, seared with passion, shivered to find herself out there in a great white light, that fell cold on her, and gave a shock to her inflamed soul." Later we read that "After a time the child, too, melted with her in the mixing-pot of moonlight, and she rested with the hills and lilies and houses, all swum together in a kind of swoon."

In this key scene of the mother's "trouble" (which must have been based on things that Lawrence later heard from his mother), the sense we get of Mrs. Morel, humiliated and enraged but in her innermost being haughtily inviolate, gives us a sense of all the power that Lawrence connected with his mother and of the power in the relationship that flowed between them. In this book he was able to recreate, for all time, the moment when the sympathetic bond between them reached its greatest intensity—and the moment when her death broke it. Ever after, Lawrence was to try to re-create this living bond, this magic sympathy, between himself and life. He often succeeded in creating an exciting and fruitful version of it—in relationship to his extraordinary wife Frieda; to a host of friends, disciples, admirers and readers throughout the world; even to his own novels and stories, essays and articles and poems and letters. Unlike Henry James, James Joyce, Marcel Proust, T. S. Eliot, Lawrence always makes you feel that not art but the quality of the lived experience is his greatest concern. That is why it is impossible to pick up anything by him without feeling revivified. Never were a writer's works more truly an allegory of his life, and no other writer with his imaginative standing has in our time written books that are so open to life. Yet one always feels in Lawrence his own vexation and disappointment at not being able to reproduce, in the full consciousness of his genius, the mutual sympathy he had experienced with his mother. One even feels about Lawrence's increasing disappointment and bitterness that it tore him apart physically, exhausted and shattered him. Wandering feverishly from continent to continent, increasingly irritable and vulnerable to every human defect and cultural complacency, he seems finally to have died for lack of another place to aim at; for lack, even, of another great fight to wage. His work itself was curiously never enough for him, for he could write so quickly, sitting anywhere under a tree, that the book seemed to fly out of his hand as soon as he had made it; and he was so much the only poet in his imaginative universe that he could not take other writers seriously enough to rejoice in his own greatness. He was searching, one feels, for something infinitely more intangible than fame, or a single person, or a "God"—he was searching for the remembered ecstasy of experience, the quality of feeling, that is even more evanescent than the people we connect with it. Lawrence kept looking for this even after he had reproduced it in *Sons and Lovers,* whose triumph as art was to give him so little lasting satisfaction. Art could not fulfill Lawrence's search, and only death could end it. But the ecstasy of a single human relationship that he tried to reproduce never congealed into a single image or idol or belief. Imaginatively, Lawrence was free; which is why his work could literally rise like a phoenix out of the man who consumed himself in his conflict with himself.

PART TWO

View Points

D. H. Lawrence

Lawrence was engaged to a school-mate and fellow teacher, Louie Burrows, during the writing of the first manuscripts of Paul Morel. The following excerpts from his letters to her reveal his alternate anxiety about and confidence in the book that became Sons and Lovers.

Letter to Louie Burrows, Eastwood, December 6, 1910

It is morning again, and she is still here. . . . I look at my mother and think "O Heaven—is this what life brings us to?" You see mother has had a devilish married life, for nearly forty years—and this is the conclusion—no relief. What ever I wrote, it could not be so awful as to write a biography of my mother. But after this—which is enough—I am going to write romance—when I have finished Paul Morel, which belongs to this.

Letter to Louie Burrows, Croydon, March 13, 1911

I have begun Paul Morel again. I am afraid it will be a terrible novel. But, if I can keep it to my idea and feeling, it will be a great one.

Letter to Louie Burrows, Croydon, May 7, 1911

I have managed my ten pages of Paul: I'm now on with the 112th. I wonder what it'll be like; at present it seems to me very rummy.

Letter to Louie Burrows, Croydon, November 3, 1911

Tonight I am going to begin Paul Morel again, for the third and last time.[1] I shall need all your prayers if I'm to get it done. It is a book the thought of which weighs heavily upon me. Say a Misericordia.

From Lawrence in Love, Letters to Louie Burrows, *ed. and with an introduction by James T. Boulton (Nottingham: Nottingham University Press, 1968), pp. 56, 83, 103, 146.*

[1] [Actually, he was to begin all over again after he met Frieda.]

After Lawrence's impetuous elopement with Frieda Weekley, he began a third draft of Sons and Lovers. *Letters to Edward Garnett, his publisher, and to old friends in England trace the heightening of his interest in the book's subject matter and form—an interest finally displaced by his declared need "to write differently."*

Letter to Edward Garnett, Austria, September 7, 1912

I am glad to be settling down, to get at [*Paul Morel*]. I am rather keen on it. I shall re-cast the first part altogether.

Letter to A. W. McLeod, Austria, September 17, 1912 (?)

Paul Morel is *better* than *The White Peacock* or *The Trespasser.* I'm inwardly very proud of it, though I haven't yet licked it into form—am still at that labour of love.

Letter to Edward Garnett, Italy, October 30, 1912

I've written 400 pages of *Paul Morel*. . . . Will *Sons and Lovers* do for a title? I've made the *book heaps* better—a million times.

Letter to Edward Garnett, Italy, November 14, 1912

I hasten to tell you I sent the MS. of the *Paul Morel* novel to Duckworth registered, yesterday. And I want to defend it, quick. I wrote it again, pruning it and shaping it and filling it in. I tell you it has got form—*form:* haven't I made it patiently, out of sweat as well as blood. It follows this idea: a woman of character and refinement goes into the lower class, and has no satisfaction in her own life. She has had a passion for her husband, so the children are born of passion, and have heaps of vitality. But as her sons grow up she selects them as lovers—first the eldest, then the second. These sons are *urged* into life by their reciprocal love of their mother—urged on and on. But when they come to manhood, they can't love, because their mother is the strongest power in their lives, and holds them. It's rather like Goethe and his mother and Frau von Stein and Christiana—As soon as the young men come into contact with women, there's a split. William gives his sex to a fribble, and his mother holds his soul. But the split kills him, because he doesn't know where he is. The next son gets a woman who fights for his soul—fights his mother. The son loves the mother—all the sons hate and are jealous of the

From The Collected Letters of D. H. Lawrence, *ed. Harry T. Moore (New York: The Viking Press, Inc.; London: William Heinemann, Ltd., 1962), I, 143, 147, 153, 160–61, 190–91, 205, 207, 234. Copyright 1932 by The Estate of D. H. Lawrence, copyright © renewed 1960 by Angelo Ravagli and C. Montague Weekley, Executors of the Estate of Frieda Lawrence Ravagli. Reprinted by permission of The Viking Press, Inc., and Laurence Pollinger, Ltd.*

father. The battle goes on between the mother and the girl, with
the son as object. The mother gradually proves stronger, because
of the tie of blood. The son decides to leave his soul in his mother's
hands, and, like his elder brother go for passion. He gets passion.
Then the split begins to tell again. But, almost unconsciously, the
mother realises what is the matter, and begins to die. The son casts off
his mistress, attends to his mother dying. He is left in the end naked
of everything, with the drift towards death.

It is a great tragedy, and I tell you I have written a great book.
It's the tragedy of thousands of young men in England. . . . I think
it was Ruskin's, and men like him.—Now tell me if I haven't worked
out my theme, like life, but always my theme. Read my novel. It's
a great novel. If *you* can't see the development—which is slow, like
growth—I can.

Letter to Edward Garnett, Italy, March 3, 1913

I finished and returned all the proofs of *Sons and Lovers*. I sup-
pose they came all right. It is rather a good novel—but if anything
a bit difficult to grip as a whole, at first. Yet it *is* a unified whole,
and I hate the dodge of putting a thick black line round the figures
to throw out the composition. Which shows I'm a bit uneasy about
it.

Letter to A. W. McLeod, Germany, May 21, 1913 (?)

Sons and Lovers comes out on the 29th. I've had just one copy—it
looks nice. If they don't fall on me for morals, it should go. It is my
best work, by far.

Letter to Helen Corke, Germany, May 29, 1913

Sons and Lovers comes out just now. I remember your telling me,
at the beginning, it would be great. I think it is so. I wonder if you
will agree.

Letter to A. W. McLeod, Italy, October 26, 1913 (?)

I felt you had gone off from me a bit, because of *Sons and Lovers*.
But one sheds one's sicknesses in books—repeats and presents again
one's emotions, to be master of them.

Letter to Edward Garnett, Italy, January 29, 1914

I have no longer the joy in creating vivid scenes, that I had in
Sons and Lovers. I don't care much more about accumulating objects
in the powerful light of emotion, and making a scene of them. I have
to write differently.

Letter to Barbara Low, England, September 11, 1916

I hated the *Psychoanalysis Review* of *Sons and Lovers*. You know I think "complexes" are vicious half-statements of the Freudians: sort of can't see wood for trees. When you've said *Mutter*-complex, you've said nothing—no more than if you called hysteria a nervous disease. Hysteria isn't nerves, a complex is not simply a sex relation: far from it.—My poor book: it was, as art, a fairly complete truth: so they carve a half lie out of it, and say *"Voilà."* Swine!

At some time in January, 1913, Lawrence sent Edward Garnett the following preface to Sons and Lovers, *telling him by postcard, "I was fearfully anxious to write a foreword to* Sons and Lovers, *and this is what I did. I am a fool—but it will amuse you." The foreword was discarded; but surely it deserves to be included here since it indicates the "philosophy" with which Lawrence himself interpreted the book.*

Foreword to Sons and Lovers.

To Edward Garnett.

John, the beloved disciple, says, "The Word was made Flesh." But why should he turn things round? The women simply go on bearing talkative sons, as an answer. "The Flesh was made Word."

For what was Christ? He was Word, or He became Word. What remains of Him? No flesh remains on earth, from Christ; perhaps some carpentry He shaped with His hands retains somewhere His flesh-print; and then His word, like His Carpentry just the object that His flesh produced, is the rest. He is Word. And the Father was Flesh. For even if it were by the Holy Ghost His spirit were begotten, yet flesh cometh only out of flesh. So the Holy Ghost must either have been, or have borne from the Father, at least one grain of flesh. The Father was Flesh—and the Son, who in Himself was finite and had form, became Word. For form is the uttered Word, and the Son is the Flesh as it utters the Word, but the unutterable Flesh is the Father.

And the Word is not spoken by the Father, who is Flesh, forever

From *The Letters of D. H. Lawrence, ed. and with an introduction by Aldous Huxley* (New York: The Viking Press; London: William Heinemann, Ltd., 1932), pp. 97–104. *Copyright 1932 by The Estate of D. H. Lawrence, copyright © renewed 1960 by Angelo Ravagli and C. Montague Weekley, Executors of the Estate of Frieda Lawrence Ravagli. Reprinted by permission of The Viking Press and Laurence Pollinger, Ltd.*

Father which, through the Son, is tossed away. It is that part of
the Flesh in the Son which is capable of spreading out thin and
wide, losing its concentration and completeness, ceasing to be a be-
getter, and becoming only a vision, a flutter of petals, God rippling
through the Son till he breaks in a laugh, called a blossom, that shines
and is gone. The vision itself, the flutter of petals, the rose, the Father
through the Son wasting himself in a moment of consciousness, consciousness of his own infinitude and gloriousness, a Rose, a Clapping
of the Hands, a Spark of Joy thrown off from the Fire to die ruddy in
red-darkness, a Snip of Flame, the Holy Ghost, the Revelation. And
this the eternal Trinity.

And God the Father, the Inscrutable, the Unknowable, we know
in the Flesh, in Woman. She is the door for our in-going and our out-
coming. In her we go back to the Father: but like the witnesses of the
Transfiguration, blind and unconscious.

Yea, like bees in and out of a hive, we come backwards and forwards
to our woman. And the Flowers of the World are Words, are Utterance—"Uttering glad leaves," Whitman said. And we are bees that
fly between, from the flowers home to the hive and the Queen; for she
is at the centre of the hive, and stands in the way of bees for God the
Father, the Almighty, the Unknowable, the Creator. In her all things
are born, both words and bees. She is the quick of all the change, the
hour, the production.

And the bee, who is a Son, comes home to his Queen as to the
Mother, in service and humility, for suggestion, and renewal, and
identification which is the height of his glory, for begetting. And again
the bee goes forth to attend the flowers, the Word in his pride and
masterfulness of new strength and new wisdom. And as he comes and
goes, so shall man for ever come and go; go to his work, his Uttering,
wherein he is masterful and proud; come home to his woman, through
whom is God the Father, and who is herself, whether she will have it
or not, God the Father, before whom the man in his hour is full of
reverence, and in whom he is glorified and hath the root of his pride.
But not only does he come and go: it is demanded of him that
he come and go. It is the systole and diastole of the Heart, that shall
not The bee comes home to the hive, and the hive expels him to attend
the flowers. The hive draws home the bee, the bee leaps off the threshold of the hive, with strength, and is gone. He carries home to the hive
the essence, of flowers, his joy in the Word he has uttered, he flies
forth again from the hive, carrying to the flowers the strength and
valour of his scrambling body, which is God Almighty in him. So he
fetches and carries, carries and fetches.
So the man comes home to woman and to God, so God the Father
receives his Son again, a man of the undying flesh; and so the man
goes forth from the house of his woman, so God expels him forth to

unquestioned and unanswerable, but by the Son. Adam was the first
Christ: not the Word made Flesh, but the Flesh made Word. Out of
the Flesh cometh the Word, and the Word is finite, as a piece of carpentry, and hath an end. But the Flesh is infinite and has no end. Out
of the Flesh cometh the Word, which blossoms for a moment and is no
more. Out of the Flesh hath come every Word, and in the Flesh lies
every Word that will be uttered. The Father is the Flesh, the eternal
and unquestionable, the law-giver but not the law; whereas the Son
is the mouth. And each law is a fabric that must crumble away, and
the Word is a graven image that is worn down, and forsaken, like the
Sphinx in the desert.

We are the Word, we are not the Flesh. The Flesh is beyond us.
And when we love our neighbour as ourself, we love that word, our
neighbour, and not that flesh. For that Flesh is not our neighbour,
it is the Father, which is in Heaven, and forever beyond our knowledge. We are the Word, we know the Word, and the Word alone
is ours. When we say "I," we mean "The Word I am." This flesh I
am is beyond me.

So that if we love our neighbour, we love that Word, our neighbour,
and we hate that Lie, our neighbour, which is a deformity. With that
Flesh, our neighbour, We, the Word-Utterer, have nothing to do. For
the Son is not greater than the Father. And if we love and subserve
that Flesh, our neighbour, which is the Father, it is only by denying
and desecrating the Father in ourselves. For the Father is the Almighty. The Flesh will feel no pain that is not upon itself, and will
know no hurt but its own destruction. But no man can destroy the
Almighty, yet he can deny Him. And pain is a denial of the Father.
If then we feel the pain and suffering of our neighbour's flesh, we are
putting destruction upon our own flesh, which is to deny and make
wrathful the Father. Which we have done. For in loving our neighbour, the Flesh, as ourself, we have said, "There is no Father, there
is only the Word." For it is the Word hath charity, not the Flesh. And
it is the Word that answereth the cry of the Word. But if the Word,
hearing a cry, shall say, "My flesh is destroyed, the bone melteth
away," that is to blaspheme the Father. For the Word is but fabric
builded of the Flesh. And when the fabric is finished, then shall the
Flesh enjoy it in its hour.

But we have said, "Within this fabric of the Word the Flesh is
held." And so, the Son has usurped the Father. And so, the Father,
which is the Flesh, withdraws from us, and the Word stands in ruins,
as Nineveh and Egypt are dead words on the plains, whence the
Flesh has withdrawn itself. For the lesser cannot contain the greater,
nor the Son contain the Father, but he is of the Father.

And it is upon the head of that nation that shall deny the Father.
For the Flesh will depart from that collective Word, the nation, and

that great nation shall remain as a Word in ruin, its own monument.

For who shall say, "No child shall be born of me and my wife. I, the Word, have said it"? And who shall say—"That woman whom my flesh, in its unquestionable sincerity, cleaveth toward, shall not come unto my flesh. But my Word shall come unto her. I, the Word have said it"? That is to usurp the flesh of my neighbour, and hold governance over it by the word. And who shall say, "That woman shall be Flesh of my Flesh. I, the Word, have said it"? For either the woman is Flesh of my Flesh, or she is not, and the Word altereth nothing, but can only submit or deny.

And when we burned the heretic at the stake, then did we love that Word, our neighbour, and hate that lie, the heretic. But we did also deny the Father, and say, "There is only Word." And when we suffer in our flesh the pangs of those that hunger, then we do deny the Flesh, and say, it is not. For the Flesh suffereth not from the hunger of the neighbour, but only from its own hunger. But the Word loveth its neighbour, and shall answer to the cry of the Word, "It is just, what thou askest." For the Word hath neither passion nor pain, but lives and moves in equity. It has charity, which we call love. But only the Flesh has love, for that is the Father, and in love he begets us all, of love are we begotten. But it was spoken, "They shall be one Flesh." Thus did the Word usurp the Father, saying, "I unite you one flesh." Whereas the Word can but confirm. For the twain are one flesh, whether the Word speak or not. And if they be not one twain, then the Word can never make them so, for the Flesh is not contained in the Word, but the Word in the Flesh. But if a man shall say, "This woman is flesh of my flesh," let him see to it that he be not blaspheming the Father. For the woman is not flesh of his flesh, by the bidding of the Word; but it is of the Father. And if he takes a woman, saying in the arrogance of the Word, "The flesh of that woman is goodly," then he has said, "The flesh of that woman is goodly as a servant unto the Word, which is me," and so hath blasphemed the Father, by which he has his being, and she hath her being. And the Flesh shall forsake these two, they shall be fabric of Word. And their race shall perish.

But if in my passion I slay my neighbour, it is no sin of mine, but it is his sin, for he should not have permitted me. But if my Word shall decide and decree that my neighbour die, then that is sin, for the Word destroyeth the Flesh, the Son blasphemeth the Father. And yet, if a man hath denied his Flesh, saying, "I, the Word, have dominion over the flesh of my neighbour," then shall the Flesh, his neighbour, slay him in self-defence. For a man may hire my Word, which is the utterance of my flesh, which is my work. But my Flesh is the Father, which is before the Son.

And so it was written: "The Word was made Flesh," lary, "And of the Flesh was made Flesh-of-the-Flesh, is again backward, and because the Son, struggling to u took for his God the accomplishment of his work, the Out of his flesh the Word had to come, and the flesh w unfathomed, so it was called the servant. And the serv vant was woman. So the Son arranged it, because he too his own work when it should be accomplished: as if a ca the chair he struggled with but had not yet made, God. is not a god, it is only a rigid image. So is the Word parallel of the chair. And so the end having been chos ginning, the whole chronology is upside-down: the Word and Man lay down and gave birth to Woman. Wherea: Woman lay in travail, and gave birth to Man, who in hi his word.

It is as if a bit of apple-blossom stood for God in hi apple was the Son, as being something more gross but s while the pip that comes out of the apple, like Adam's r secondary produce, that is spat out, and which, if it falls just happens to start the process of apple-tree going a little pip that one spits out has in it all the blossom well as all the tree, the leaves, the perfume, the drop: heaven knows what else that we never see, contained by bit of white flesh: and the tree, the leaves, the flowers t the apple are only amplifications of this little seed, spen has amplified itself enough, but can go on to other petalled flowers and little brown apples, if we did but

So we take the seed as the starting point in this cycle. the Flesh. She produces all the rest of the flesh, includ mediary pieces called man—and these curious pieces c like stamens that can turn into exquisite-coloured po they can beat out the stuff of their life thin, thin, thin, t or a purple petal, or a thought, or a Word. And when out that it ceases to be begetting stuff, of the Father, but wider, expanded and showy: then we say, "This is the everybody will agree that a rose is only a rose because and that the rose is the utmost of all that flow of life, But what is really "Rose" is only in that quivering, shi of flesh which is the same, unchanged for ever, a co called if you like rodoplasm, the eternal, the unque infinite of the Rose, the Flesh, the Father—which were the Mother.

So there is the Father—which should be called Mot Son, who is the Utterer, and then the Word. And the W

waste himself in utterance, in work, which is only God the Father realizing himself in a moment of forgetfulness. Thus the eternal working. And it is joy enough to see it, without asking why. For it is as if the Father took delight in seeing himself for a moment unworking, for a moment wasting himself that he might know himself. For every petalled flower, which alone is a Flower, is a work of productiveness. It is a moment of joy, of saying, "I am I." And every table or chair a man makes is a self-same waste of his life, a fixing into stiffness and deadness of a moment of himself, for the sake of the glad cry: "This is I—I am I." And this glad cry, when we know, is the Holy Ghost, the Comforter.

So, God Eternal, the Father, continues, doing we know not what, not why: we only know He is. And again and again comes the exclamation of joy or of pain which is joy—like Galileo and Shakespeare and Darwin—which announces "I am I."

And in the woman is the eternal continuance, and from the man, in the human race, comes the exclamation of joy and astonishment at new self-revelation, revelation of that which is woman to a man.

Now every woman, according to her kind, demands that a man shall come home to her with joy and weariness of the work he has done during the day: that he shall then while he is with her, be re-born of her; that in the morning he shall go forth with his new strength.

But if the man does not come home to a woman, leaving her to take account of him, but is a stranger to her; if when he enters her house, he does not become simply her man of flesh, entered into her house as if it were her greater body, to be warmed, and restored, and nourished, from the store the day has given her, then she shall expel him from her house, as a drone. It is as inevitable as the working of the bees, as that a stick shall go down stream.

For in the flesh of the woman does God exact Himself. And out of the flesh of the woman does He demand: "Carry this of Me forth to utterance." And if the man deny, or be too weak, then shall the woman find another man, of greater strength. And if, because of the Word, which is the Law, she do not find another man nor he another woman, then shall they both be destroyed. For he, to get that rest and warmth, and nourishment which he should have had from her, his woman, must consume his own flesh and so destroy himself: whether with wine, or other kindling. And she, either her surplus shall wear away her flesh, in sickness, or in lighting up and illuminating old dead Words, or she shall spend it in fighting with her man to make him take her, or she shall turn to her son, and say, "Be you my Go-between."

But the man who is the go-between from Woman to Production is the lover of that woman. And if that Woman be his mother then is he her lover in part only; he carries for her, but is never received into her for his confirmation and renewal, and so wastes himself away in the flesh. The old son-lover was Œdipus. The name of the new one is legion. And if a son-lover take a wife, then is she not his wife, she is only his bed. And his life will be torn in twain, and his wife in her despair shall hope for sons, that she may have her lover in her hour.

Frieda Lawrence

Letter to Edward Garnett, September 1912 (?)

I think Lawrence quite missed the point in *Paul Morel*. He really loved his mother more than anybody, even with his other women, real love, a sort of Oedipus; his mother must have been adorable. He is writing P.M. again, reads bits to me and we fight like blazes over it, he is so often beside the point, "but 'I'll learn him to be a toad' as the boy said as he stamped on the toad."

Letter to Edward Garnett [postscript and date missing]

I also feel as if I ought to say something about L.'s formlessness. I don't think he has no form. I used to. But now I think anybody must see in *Paul Morel* the hang of it. The mother is really the thread, the domineering note.

Letter to Edward Garnett, February 1914 (?)

[*Sons and Lovers*] is a failure but you must feel something at the back of it struggling, trying to come out. You see, I don't really believe in *Sons and Lovers;* it feels as if there were nothing *behind* all those happenings as if there were no *"Hinterland der Seele,"* only intensely felt fugitive things. I who am a believer though I don't know in what, to me it seems an irreligious book. It does not seem the deepest and last thing said; if for instance a man loves in a book the pretty curl on the neck of "her," he loves it ever so intensely and beautifully, there is something behind that curl, *more* than that curl; there is *she,* the living striving *she.* Writers are so beside the point, not *direct* enough.

Letter to Edward Garnett, May 1913 (?)

I only just realized the amazing brutality of *Sons and Lovers.* How that brutality remains ["remains" a correction by D. H. L. of her "is"

From *Frieda Lawrence,* The Memoirs and Correspondence, *ed. E. W. Tedlock (London: William Heinemann, Ltd., 1961), pp. 185, 202, 196. Reprinted by permission of Alfred A. Knopf, Inc., and Laurence Pollinger, Ltd.*

and his own "is there": Tedlock's note] in spite of Christianity, of the two thousand years. . . . Paul says to his mother, when she is dying, "If I'd got to die, I would be quick about it, I would *will* to die." Doesn't it seem awful! Yet, one *does* feel like that.

Edward Garnett

Mr. Lawrence silenced . . . critics [of *The White Peacock* and *The Trespasser*] by his third novel, *Sons and Lovers,* an epic of family life in a colliery district, a piece of social history on a large canvas, painted with a patient thoroughness and bold veracity which both Balzac and Flaubert might have envied. The central theme, an unhappy working-class marriage, a woman's struggle to rear her children while sustained by her strong puritanical spirit, develops later into a study of her maternal aversion to surrendering her son to another woman's arms. The theme is dissected in its innermost spiritual fibres with an unflinching and loving exactitude, while the family drama is seen against an impressive background of the harsh, driving realities of life in a colliery district. This novel is really the only one of any breadth of vision in contemporary English fiction that lifts working-class life out of middle-class hands, and restores it to its native atmosphere of hard veracity. The mining people, their mental outlook, ways of life, and habits, and the woof of their domestic joys and cares, are contrasted with some country farming types in a neighbourhood village, where the smoky horizon of industrialism merges, to the passionate eyes of a girl and boy in love, in the magic of quiet woods and pastures. The whole treatment is unerringly true and spiritually profound, marred a little by a feeling of photographic accuracy in the narrative and by a lack of restraint in some of the later love scenes.

From Friday Nights, *by Edward Garnett (New York: Alfred A. Knopf, Inc., 1922), pp. 154–55. Copyright 1922 by Alfred A. Knopf, Inc., and renewed 1950 by David Garnett. Reprinted by permission of the publisher.*

Wyndham Lewis

(1) The Unconscious; (2) The Feminine; (3) The Communist; those are the main principles of action of the mind of Mr. [D. H.] Lawrence, linked in a hot and piping trinity of rough-stuff primitiv-

From Wyndham Lewis, *Paleface, The Philosophy of the "Melting-Pot" (London: Chatto and Windus, 1929), pp. 180–81. Reprinted by permission of Mrs. A. Wyndham Lewis.*

ism, and freudian hot-sex-stuff. With *Sons and Lovers*, his first book, he was at once hot-foot upon the fashionable trail of incest; the book is an eloquent wallowing mass of Mother-love and Sex-idolatry. His *Women in Love* is again the same thick, sentimental, luscious stew. . . . The motif of the "child-cult," which is usually found prominently in any "revolutionary" mixture, is echoed, and indeed screamed, wept and bellowed, throughout *Sons and Lovers*.

Ernest Seillière

In Lawrence's first important novel, *Sons and Lovers*, vitality in the male does not yet take the place of all other virtues, for the miner Morel, father of the protagonist, is amply endowed with that natural quality but it fails to earn for him either the lasting love of his wife or the respect of his sons. When he is young, he is handsome, seductive, amiable, charming: not in the least intellectual, of course, but radiant with a warm, winsome gaiety. The flamboyant sensuality of the man, with his sad, golden sweetness, his vitality which leaps from his flesh like a flame from a hearth, is not dimmed by the brooding spirit that animates his wife so that he seems to her at first a marvel, a pure marvel, "beyond her." But the wife's illusions do not last long; she is soon forced to despise him for his bad behavior. Then, puritan in her own upbringing, she sets herself the the task of making him "moral": she tries to force him to face the consequences of his actions.—What an intolerable responsibility for the mother of a family!—He cannot endure it for it drives him "out of his mind."

Morel, evidence affirms, is a portrait of Lawrence's father. But Lawrence who as a writer had not yet adopted[1] a theoretical or even messianic ideology as he was drawing this faithful portrait and who, besides, wrote from bitter personal experience, does not make a hero of his pub-crawler. The moral shiftlessness and brutality of the miner make his sons begin to hate him. . . . It is in this most unsympathetic fashion that the [Lawrentian] male, favorite of the goddess Life, makes his *début* in a fictive world that comes to be eloquent with him; but the ultimate passional experience of Lawrence—and that which he saw in himself as vitality, the sign of special Natural gifts— were rapidly to change his views of the male [principle]. To his Aaron [in *Aaron's Rod*], a Morel scarcely less brutal and quite as conscienceless, he would seem to give utter approval a few years later!

From David-Herbert Lawrence et les Récentes Idéologies Allemandes *by Ernest Seillière (Paris: Boivin et Cie., 1936), pp. 176–78. Editor's translation.*

[1] [M. Seillière's actual phrase is "had not yet been *overrun* by . . . ," etc. (italics mine).]

Karl Menninger

It is important to emphasize that fixations of any type are determined more by hating and fearing than by love, and that they only masquerade as love. One might say that persons who have "a mother fixation" fear their mothers more than their fathers; they fear to leave the mother either for a passive, submissive relation to the father which brings them into competition with the mother, or for active masculine interest in available women. The mother is safe as a love object because she is not accessible. By a pretense of attachment to her such a boy can conceal his hostility to her, eliminate the necessity of any fear of her, and avoid the consequences of attempting to express his masculinity in a normal way. (D. H. Lawrence described this classically in *Sons and Lovers*.) It is really more pathological to be thus passively attached to the mother than to be passively attached to the father, because it is a more infantile, parasitic relationship and therefore contains a larger element of hostility and a smaller component of real object love. But both represent essentially a repudiation of masculine aims and character.

From Love Against Hate, *by Karl Menninger (New York: Harcourt, Brace and Company, 1942), p. 57. Reprinted by permission of the publisher.*

Mark Schorer

To say what one means in art is never easy, and the more intimately one is implicated in one's material, the more difficult it is. If, besides, one commits fiction to a therapeutic function which is to be operative not on the audience but on the author, declaring, as D. H. Lawrence did, that "One sheds one's sicknesses in books, repeats and presents again one's emotions to be master of them," the difficulty is vast. It is an acceptable theory only with the qualification that technique, which objectifies, is under no other circumstances so imperative. For merely to repeat one's emotions, merely to look into one's heart and write, is also merely to repeat the round of emotional bondage. If our books are to be exercises in self-analysis, then technique must—and alone can—take the place of the absent analyst. . . .

[*Sons and Lovers*] has two themes: the crippling effects of a mother's love on the emotional development of her son; and the "split" between kinds of love, physical and spiritual, which the son develops,

From Mark Schorer, *"Technique as Discovery."* The Hudson Review, I, No. I (Spring 1948), 75–78. Reprinted by permission of Farrar, Straus & Giroux, Inc., and A. M. Heath & Company, Ltd.

the kinds represented by two young women, Clara and Miriam. The two themes should, of course, work together, the second being, actually, the result of the first: this "split" is the "crippling." So one would expect to see the novel developed, and so Lawrence, in his famous letter to Edward Garnett,[1] where he says that Paul is left at the end with the "drift towards death," apparently thought he had developed it. Yet in the last few sentences of the novel, Paul rejects his desire for extinction and turns towards "the faintly humming, glowing town," to life—as nothing in his previous history persuades us that he could unfalteringly do.

The discrepancy suggests that the book may reveal certain confusions between intention and performance.

The first of these is the contradiction between Lawrence's explicit characterizations of the mother and father and his tonal evaluations of them. It is a problem not only of style (of the contradiction between expressed moral epithets and the more general texture of the prose which applies to them) but of point of view. Morel and Lawrence are never separated, which is a way of saying that Lawrence maintains for himself in this book the confused attitude of his character. The mother is a "proud, *honorable* soul," but the father has a "small, *mean* head." This is the sustained contrast; the epithets are characteristic of the whole; and they represent half of Lawrence's feelings. But what is the other half? Which of these characters is given his real sympathy—the hard, self-righteous, aggressive, demanding mother who comes through to us, or the simple, direct, gentle downright fumbling, ruined father? There are two attitudes here. Lawrence (and Morel) loves his mother, but he also hates her for compelling his love; and he hates his father with the true Freudian jealousy, but he also loves him for what he is in himself, and he sympathizes more deeply with him because his wholeness has been destroyed by the mother's domination, just as his, Lawrence-Morel's, has been.

This is a psychological tension which disrupts the form of the novel and obscures its meaning, because neither the contradiction in style nor the confusion in point of view is made to right itself. Lawrence is merely repeating his emotions, and he avoids an austerer technical scrutiny of his material because it would compel him to master them. He would not let the artist be stronger than the man.

The result is that, at the same time that the book condemns the mother, it justifies her; at the same time that it shows Paul's failure, it offers rationalizations which place the failure elsewhere. The handling of the girl, Miriam, if viewed closely, is pathetic in what it signifies for Lawrence, both as man and artist. For Miriam is made the mother's scape-goat, and in a different way from the way that she was in life. The central section of the novel is shot through with alternate

[1] [Pp. 86–87 of this volume.]

statements as to the source of the difficulty: Paul is unable to love Miriam wholly, and Miriam can love only his spirit. The contradictions appear sometimes within single paragraphs, and the point of view is never adequately objectified and sustained to tell us which is true. The material is never seen as material; the writer is caught in it exactly as firmly as he was caught in his experience of it. "That's how women are with me," said Paul. "They want me like mad, but they don't want to belong to me." So he might have said, and believed it; but at the end of the novel, Lawrence is still saying that, and himself believing it.

For the full history of this technical failure, one must read *Sons and Lovers* carefully and then learn the history of the manuscript from the book called *D. H. Lawrence: A Personal Record*, by one E. T., who was Miriam in life. The basic situation is clear enough. The first theme—the crippling effects of the mother's love—is developed right through to the end; and then suddenly, in the last few sentences, turns on itself, and Paul gives himself to life, not death. But all the way through, the insidious rationalizations of the second theme have crept in to destroy the artistic coherence of the work. A "split" would occur in Paul; but as the split is treated, it is superimposed upon rather than developed in support of the first theme. It is a rationalization made from it. If Miriam is made to insist on spiritual love, the meaning and the power of theme one are reduced; yet Paul's weakness is disguised. Lawrence could not separate the investigating analyst, who must be objective, from Lawrence, the subject of the book; and the sickness was not healed, the emotion not mastered, the novel not perfected. All this, and the character of a whole career, would have been altered if Lawrence had allowed his technique to discover the fullest meaning of his subject.

Father William Tiverton (Martin Jarrett-Kerr)

In a letter to Garnett about *Sons and Lovers* in 1912[1] Lawrence describes the novel and says that the hero of it "is left in the end naked of everything, with the drift towards death." Now this is interesting. For from the last pages of the novel itself we should not have gained quite that impression. True, much of Paul is still bound to his dead mother—as we see from the rather maudlin poem "The Virgin Mother":

From Father William Tiverton (Martin Jarrett-Kerr), D. H. Lawrence and Human Existence (London: SCM Press, 1961), pp. 47–49. Copyright © 1961 by SCM Press. Reprinted by permission of the author and the publisher.

[1] [Pp. 86–87 of this volume.]

And so, my love, my mother,
I shall always be true to you.
Twice I am born, my dearest,
To life, and to death, in you;
And this is the life hereafter
Wherein I am true. . . .

Is the last word now uttered
Is the farewell said?
Spare me the strength to leave you
Now you are dead.
I must go, but my soul lies helpless
Beside your bed.

But by the time he actually comes to write the last paragraphs of the novel he has stepped a little further out of Paul Morel:

His soul could not leave her, wherever she was. Now she was gone abroad into the night and he was with her still. They were together . . . "Mother!" he whispered—"mother" . . . . But no, he would not give in. Turning sharply, he walked towards the city's phosphorescence. His fists were shut, his mouth set fast. He would not take that direction, to the darkness, to follow her. He walked towards the faintly humming, glowing town, quickly.

It is really Miriam who has the "drift towards death." As they go out of his room, to part for ever:

How bitter, how unutterably bitter, it made her that he rejected her sacrifice! Life ahead looked dead, as if the glow were gone out. . . . She waited for him, took the flowers, and they went out together, he talking, she feeling dead.

Writers on Lawrence have, it seems to me, much exaggerated his Oedipus complex. The mother-attachment once shaken off, Paul Morel once dead, he does grow into a separate existence which cannot be interpreted in terms of Mrs. Lawrence. True, there are occasional echoes of it later. It recurs again, for instance, at Miss Frost's death in *The Lost Girl:* "Alvina knew death—which is untellable. She knew that her darling carried away a portion of her own soul into death." But this is only faint. Had it been stronger it would have surely appeared in *The Rainbow* and its sequel, where there would have been plenty of scope for a "Mrs. Morel-Paul" theme. But whereas there are hints of the relationship between Lawrence's father and mother in Tom Brangwen and Lydia Lensky (Lydia's first marriage to the Pole has an echo of Mrs. Lawrence's first love before she met the father of D. H.), there is very little of the possessive motherhood anywhere. In the superb first three chapters of *The Rainbow* (among the greatest Lawrence ever wrote) there is the search for—and discovery of—a satisfactory relationship such as the Morel-Lawrence family lacked.

Frank O'Connor

When we look at the last complete period of the novel, we find such names as Marcel Proust, James Joyce, André Gide, D. H. Lawrence, E. M. Forster, Thomas Mann, and Virginia Woolf.

And we are at once pulled up because at least four of the principal figures did not write novels at all. They wrote autobiography more or less thinly disguised as fiction. Another characteristic of this quartet is that none of them seems to have been sexually normal. All fell deeply under the influence of their mothers; Gide and Proust remained homosexual for their entire lives; Lawrence showed strongly marked homosexual tendencies, while Joyce's work covers practically every known form of sexual deviation. The only subject that none of them could apparently treat was normal heterosexual love.

Now, this can scarcely be a coincidence, and when we examine their work and find that even the types of deviation resemble one another, we are forced to the conclusion that there must be a common element that makes their authors react in this particular way.

Let us look first at Lawrence's *Sons and Lovers,* which is particularly interesting because, though it ends as a novel of the modern type, it begins as one of the classical kind, made familiar to us by nineteenth-century novelists.

To begin with, we have to notice that it is the work of one of the New Men who are largely a creation of the Education Act of 1870. Besides, we must note that it comes from the English Midlands, the industrial area. Naturally, the two facts are linked, and they represent a cultural shift not only from the middle to the working class, but also from the area of wealth to the area of industry. The young people in the book are full of literary allusions that are not merely the self-conscious showing off of a young literary man, but represent the whole struggle of the working classes for culture. There is the same atmosphere in C. P. Snow's *Strangers and Brothers,* and for a similar reason.

It indicates too the dangers of such a shift of attitudes, for the Midlands, at least to a foreigner like myself, seem to be a different country altogether from the South of England, and even at times to resemble Ireland more than England. They are dissenting in religion,

From The Mirror in the Roadway, *by Frank O'Connor (New York: Alfred A. Knopf, Inc., 1956), pp. 270–78. Copyright © 1956 by Frank O'Connor. Reprinted by permission of Alfred A. Knopf, Inc., and A. D. Peters & Company.*

socialist in politics, and with a way of life which—again to a foreigner —seems full of dignity and even beauty. And, again, it is worth remembering that one of Lawrence's best stories, *Odour of Chrysanthemums,* which describes a miner's death, is not only quite unlike any other English story: though the critics have failed to notice it, it is also a very careful pastiche of Synge's *Riders to the Sea.* It suggests that young people of Lawrence's period did apparently recognize that in some ways their life was closer to Irish than to English ways, and that if it was to be given its full dignity, it had to be approached from an Irish standpoint.

But—and this is Lawrence's tragedy—it reminds us too that, unlike Ireland, the Midlands have no cultural capital, and that a young man of genius is necessarily driven to London, where he may learn only too quickly to despise the standards of his own people. This is not true of everybody, but of Lawrence it certainly is true. London acquaintances thought him something of a bounder and a cad. The family described under the name of Leivers in *Sons and Lovers* certainly did not think him either. It is the tragedy of William in the same novel. In later years Lawrence is the homeless, rootless man of letters drifting from country to country, continent to continent, writing with unfailing energy and brilliance, but never with the intensity displayed in *Sons and Lovers* and some of his early stories.

The break with his roots occurred during the writing of the novel, and it is plain for anyone who will take the trouble to read it carefully. Absolutely, the opening half is the greatest thing in English fiction. It has all the brilliance of *Pride and Prejudice* and the opening of *Middlemarch* with the tragic power of certain scenes in *The Last Chronicle.* Put in its simplest form, it is the dilemma of a sensitive boy between the conflicting claims of mother and sweetheart. This adds a new element of tragedy to the novel, for, despite the universal quality of the theme, it is an element that could only have come from the New Men and the industrial areas, for it is only in those surroundings that a boy is forced to recognize the spiritual achievement of motherhood. A hundred pounds a year would have been sufficient to mask the whole achievement and tragedy of Mrs. Morel. Even a difference in class would have done so, for, greatly as Mrs. Crawley is drawn by Trollope, her struggle is presented as it appeared to a member of the upper classes: a sordid, unnecessary, *imposed* ordeal. In Lawrence, poverty is treated as a necessary condition of life, and it is by means of the explicit exiguous budgets that we are made to appreciate the full significance of Mrs. Morel's attempts to create order and beauty about her, and the delight and anguish these could bring to a sensitive boy. We *respect* Mrs. Crawley's struggle to find necessities for her family; we *rejoice* in the glorious scene in which Mrs. Morel gives rein to her wicked extravagance and comes home clutching a pot that cost her fivepence and a bunch of pansies and daisies that cost her fourpence.

Again it is the Midland background that gives significance to Miriam's passion for culture, this, too, a struggle toward the light, though of a different kind. As we are made to feel the weight of Morel's physical violence and the brutality of the mines crushing us down like a leaden sky, so too we feel with almost agonizing intensity the upward movement in chapel, school, and home, the passion of desire to "build Jerusalem in England's green and pleasant land." Nature is not, as in Hardy, a dark background to a gloomy fate, but an upward surging like music, poetry, religion. No other novel is so filled with flowers. When in a novel for the leisured classes someone talks of Rilke, or a Picasso print, or carnations, one's tendency is to groan: "Holy Smoke, he's off again!" But we rejoice in Mrs. Morel's little triumph over the potman, in Miriam's algebra lesson, in Mrs. Morel's three little bulbs under the hedge. These are no longer the negatives of dandyism or the neutrals of an educated class, but the positive achievements of a life with a sense of purpose and direction, lived by people who are complete moral entities. . . .

It is hard to criticize this matchless book, yet there *is* something wrong with it, and, whatever it may be, it is the same thing that is wrong with Lawrence himself and that turns him into a homeless man of letters, and it is here, under our eyes, that the smash occurs if only we could see what it is. What I mean is not a literary fault, or is so only in a secondary sense. It would be only natural that a young man's book should contain shifting planes, particularly when all the significant scenes are written with such explosive power that it is a miracle when he recovers any sense of direction at all. No, the smash is a psychological one and inherent in the situation that he describes rather than in the technique he uses to describe it. It is inherent in the situation of the young man torn between his mother and Miriam, both of whom want the same thing from him.

There is almost certainly a false note in the chapters describing Miriam as Paul Morel's mistress. I do not know if in real life Lawrence was actually the lover of the girl he describes as Miriam, nor am I greatly concerned about the question. But the situation of the novel implies that they could never have been lovers, and that this was in fact the thing that drove Paul to Clara. . . . Human love—the type represented by Miriam—is bound to represent a betrayal of the mother, because the love is identical except for this one slight specialized thing. Miriam is his mother's rival because the love that she offers is human love; Clara is not because the love that she offers is in fact a non-human love.

Clara is non-human in the same way as every single woman whom Lawrence described after the writing of this book is non-human. None of them is allowed to challenge the image of his mother in humanity.

And this is where we come to the really pathological streak in the book. Clara is a married woman whose husband is a smith in the surgical-appliance store where Paul is employed, and immediately she appears in the novel her husband appears also. He hates Paul long before Paul becomes the lover of his wife. When Paul and she become friendly, Paul presses her with questions about her relations with Dawes. He even has a fight with Dawes, and later goes to visit him in the hospital and makes friends with him. The two men have a peculiar relationship centered on their common possession of Clara, and finally Paul brings about the reunion of husband and wife.

Now, these chapters, which occupy a considerable part of the last half of the book, have nothing whatever to do with the subject of the novel—at least on the surface. They might easily belong to an entirely different novel. Indeed, they might be about different characters, for from this point onward Paul is referred to as "Morel," a name which has so far been associated only with his father, so that we even get superficially confused in our reading. Lawrence's original intention is fairly clear. It was to present Miriam not as a type of human love, but as a type of spiritual love, Clara as a type of sensual love, neither of which can satisfy the heart of the young man who loves his mother. This design has been obscured by the irrelevant physical relations with Miriam on the one hand, and on the other by the emphasis laid on Clara's husband as opposed to Clara herself. But that is only part of the trouble. The real trouble is that Paul Morel is not in love with Clara, but with Dawes. . . .

It is hard to know what the real origin of this perverse attraction in Lawrence represents. That it existed in him in real life we may safely deduce from Murry's remark—made in all innocence of the meaning of the texts I have quoted—that Lawrence was attracted to Frieda's husband almost as much as to Frieda. Obviously the attraction is homosexual, but that word is so loosely and coarsely abused that it can scarcely be applied without misgivings to a noble and refined personality like Lawrence's. It is certainly linked with his adoration of his mother, and it seems as though the link must be a specialized form of sexuality which excludes the spiritual element merely because it would then become a rival to mother love. At the same time, the figure of the father, consciously excluded by the boy, would seem to return in an unrecognizable, unconscious form and take its place in the relationship with the woman. If one accepts this reading of it (and it is as tentative as any reading of an analogical situation must be), Dawes is really Paul's father, and Paul, through his relationship with Clara, which gives him the opportunity of probing Dawes's relations with his wife, is not only able to repeat the offense against his father by robbing him of his wife, but is also, in the manner of a fairy tale, able to undo the wrong by reconciling them.

It is a beautiful example of the dual function of such analogical relationships.

Whatever the origin of the situation, it is the key to Lawrence's later work. His rejection of Miriam is a rejection of masculinity in himself, and after it he is condemned to write only of those things which the feminine side of his character permits him to write of. He is an intuitive writer by sheer necessity. To Edward Garnett he defended his new, non-human form of writing by the pretense that the old sort of realistic writing which Garnett understood was out of date, but that his own choice of this sort of writing took place only after *Sons and Lovers* is clearly untrue. The choice was made during the actual writing, and the result is the Clara-Dawes section, the end of the old Lawrence and the beginning of the new.

Kingsley Widmer

In the concluding scene [of *Sons and Lovers*] the now rootless and despairing hero makes a final rejection of childhood sweetheart, his home, and his past. It is a near total negation, and not an affirmation of anything else—his art has been abandoned; his later love has, with a peculiar sexual twist, been disposed of; and he has no other purpose. He is thinking to himself that he must "stop all this restlessness and beating against death," but he cannot, and "in the vastness and terror of the immense night . . . which will remain at last eternal," the hero finds himself "at core a nothingness. . . ." While he resists the childish longing to take a shortcut to death and follow his mother, he concludes by staying isolated, rootless, purposeless, and unfulfilled. The turn in the night toward "the faintly humming, glowing town" is a negative image to Lawrence, who hated cities and towns from start to finish. The most that can be said for the hero is that, good Lawrencean, he will continue to beat restlessly against the annihilating limits. He aptly stated the theme earlier in the book: "Some sort of perversity in our souls . . . makes us not want, get away from, the very thing we want."

From The Art of Perversity, D. H. Lawrence's Shorter Fiction, *by Kingsley Widmer (Seattle: University of Washington Press, 1962), pp. 225–26, fn. 25. Copyright © 1962 by the University of Washington Press. Reprinted by permission of the publisher.*

Appendix: Selections from the May Chambers Holbrook Papers

Of the many recollections of D. H. Lawrence written by his friends, those of Mrs. May Chambers Holbrook have special value for readers of Sons and Lovers. *May Holbrook (1883–1955) was the elder sister of Jessie Chambers Wood, Lawrence's "Miriam Leivers." Like Jessie, she played, read, argued, and walked with "Bert" Lawrence during their adolescence. Unlike Jessie's, her relationship with him—what her husband Bill called that of brother and sister—was not so intense as to inhibit the objective description of his behavior which characterizes her memoirs. Having met Lawrence first when she was eleven and he about nine, Mrs. Holbrook last saw him in 1912 before his elopement with Frieda Weekley and before the Holbrooks emigrated to Canada. Their final correspondence is dated 1914, shortly after the publication of* Sons and Lovers. *The manuscript from which the excerpts below have been selected was discovered by chance in 1956. It seems to have been begun around 1934, either before or after Mrs. Holbrook read her sister's* D. H. Lawrence: A Personal Record *(1935).*

Mrs. Holbrook's reminiscences are remarkable in several ways. They keep silence, first of all, on the subject of Jessie's love for the young Lawrence. She is represented merely as a close school-mate solicitous of his health, while her mother ("Mrs. Leivers" in Sons and Lovers) *is reported to have hoped her girls would never marry this engaging firebrand who could illumine the world but would, she thought, sorely hurt a wife. The strained lessons Paul Morel gives Miriam in both algebra and heartbreak do not appear in Mrs. Holbrook's memoirs. Rather she and Bert (only later, Jessie) do their homework with a minimum of Lawrence "shouting," later roaming the farm's orchards where Bert, like Paul, shows an uncommon ecstasy at nature. The pervading tone of the Holbrook account is matter-of-fact; however, like many of Lawrence's female friends, May Holbrook musters a narrative clarity and a somewhat clinical awareness (implemented, perhaps, by hindsight,* Sons and Lovers, *and her sister's book) that make her views of the young Lawrence useful. Although it was Jessie's confessed custom never to contradict Bert, May had no such scruples. She enjoyed seeing how he would react in situations he disliked: being in the company of men alone, for example, whose sports and con-*

versation he, unlike Paul Morel who seeks out Edgar, found rough. As they matured, she played antagonist to his heretical opinions, to his preference for frivolous women instead of serious ones, and, especially, to his callous treatment of his father whose cordiality she admired.

Mrs. Holbrook's papers are rich for readers of Sons and Lovers, *for they explore characters and events significant in that book. Lydia Lawrence, in black, "disillusioned" and "plodding" (in this case, Mrs. Holbrook's language may be influenced by Lawrence's), is a far less distinguished figure than Gertrude Morel. It is her acerbity, money-fears, and maternal selfishness that dominate the Holbrook image of Lawrence's mother and none of the amiable radiance and only a little of the pity that transfigures her son's. Yet here, in an outsider's view, are Mrs. Lawrence's reactions to the stenographer Gypsy Dennis—prototype of the "Gypsy" of* Sons and Lovers; *to her high flying son William Ernest's ("William Morel"'s) engagement; and to his death which, like William's in* Sons and Lovers, *follows a trip to the hometown fair. Here is Bert Lawrence's joy in the Haggs farm. Here, too, are accounts of the temperamental differences between the patient, sociable Chambers family and the lively, caustic Lawrences whose soirées of theatrical games, reading, drawing, and wincing at Mrs. Lawrence's diatribes against sons marrying never included the miner father. Finally, Mrs. Holbrook describes the days of Mrs. Lawrence's dying which, in effect, broke Lawrence's ties to May and Jessie but which seem to have drawn from him the self-knowledge to become an artist instead of a suicide.*

The excerpts below are, regrettably, only a slight portion of the manuscript edited by Edward Nehls in his Composite Biography *of* Lawrence. *They are included here to encourage readers of* Sons and Lovers *to consult the whole text and to suggest that, though continents separate the poet from the usual diarist, memoirs like May Chambers Holbrook's help us see what the artist Lawrence had to start with: the painful baggage with which flight is earned.*

[Mrs. Lawrence] was a short, robust woman with a heavy, plodding step, her thick hair greying, shrewd grey eyes, and a kindly smile. She drooped slightly, and carried her head bent to one side a little, as if weary and discouraged. Her black dress and the apron tied around her waist bore signs of work about which she complained and

Chosen from D. H. Lawrence: A Composite Biography, *gathered, arranged, and edited by Edward Nehls (Madison: The University of Wisconsin Press, 1959), pp. 554, 557-58, 558-59, 567-68, 570, 573-74, 578, 583-84, 595-96, 618-19, 620. Copyright © 1959 by the Regents of the University of Wisconsin. Reprinted by permission of the publisher.*

was rebellious. Her expression changed swiftly from the sympathetic to the combative. In Chapel she sat at the entrance of their pew. She wore a small black bonnet with the ribbons tied very neatly, sitting with downcast eyes, her head slightly on one side. Her eldest son [George Arthur] was dark and quiet looking, his brother [William Ernest] was brilliant with flashing eyes and teeth, and unruly, tawny hair. He was popular with the night-school boys to whom he taught shorthand and with the athletes. He had an irresistible smile and seemed to find difficulty in sitting still so long, so he took down the sermon in shorthand sometimes. There were the two sisters [Emily and Ada] between whom Bert was sandwiched. Only on very rare occasions did I see the father in Chapel. He looked handsome in a rugged way: black curly hair and beard streaked slightly with silver; blue eyes smiling kindly in a rugged face, glancing over the congregation with a friendly air; well-built and strong in figure; and a genial manner. By comparison the mother appeared bitter, disillusioned, and austere. Her attire was black, as I recall it. . . .

One dull, heavy morning [1898] I came upon mother and son at the end of [their] entry. I thought Mrs. Lawrence must have a headache. Her elbow was on the coping stone on the low wall, her head resting on her hand. In her black dress and soiled apron she impressed me as one in deep misery.

Bert came a few steps to meet me, and said in a tense voice:

"I've won that scholarship."

My eyes and mouth opened in speechless admiration, and his face suddenly shone with joy, then clouded with anxiety.

"She's wondering if she'll let me go. I hope she does. I want to go."

The mother didn't change her position, but stared out over the wide valley as she said: "I don't know what to do, child. He's told you they both won the scholarship."

The other boy had been forgotten. I hardly knew him. I said I was glad, and asked when would High School start? She had not altered her position, and stared over our heads to far tree-clad hills.

"I don't know that I shall let him go."

Bert stood digging the toes of one foot in the dust, hanging his head, and said tensely, "You will let me go. I know you will."

"Oh, shall I?" she queried tartly.

"Yes, you will," he repeated very low and vibrant. "I know you will."

She stepped away from the wall and shook and tossed her head.

"Aye, if I can pinch it out of the pennies, he knows I'll let him go. He knows, oh, he knows right enough." Bert glanced with a face puckered with varying emotions, and she continued, appealing to me, "It takes money, doesn't it, child?"

But Bert broke in, "There is some money found, Mother."

"Aye, my lad, there's a little found, but there's a lot wants finding. Why, look at his clothes and boots and dinners and train fare and books."

"There's enough for books and train fare and a little more, I think, and I can wear my Sunday suit boots," he arranged eagerly.

"And they won't wear out? And what will you wear for Sunday? Tell me that. Oh, I don't know!"

And she turned up to the entry with her weary step and her shoulders a little more bowed.

"Skimp, skimp, I'm tired of skimping."

The next time I went, it was all settled that somehow means should be found for Bert to attend the High School at Nottingham.

Somewhere about this time the Lawrences took me into their parlour to show me a photograph of the girl engaged to the handsome auburn-haired brother Ernest. He was bringing her home for the holidays, and the elder sister declared:

"We're going to tidivate everything up. This parlour's going to be done so that you'll hardly know it."

"There's a lot she says is going to be done that won't get done, varnishing and such like," declared the mother.

"Well, we shall have to—" began the daughter, but the mother broke in.

"We shall have to do just as far as the money goes and that's all! That's as much as you can do, isn't it, child?" she said to me. "Besides, what's good enough for us is good enough for them who's coming."

We turned to the photograph again.

"She's nice, isn't she!" said Bert, quivering with excitement, and I said she was handsome.

" 'Handsome is as handsome does,' we shall see!" said the mother, grimly,

The sister pointed to the family group, saying, "That's him."

"Fool!" ejaculated the mother. "She knows him, don't you, child? Aye, I wonder how he's changed," she said mournfully. "They're never the same men once they go out into the world. You lose them—you might as well never have had them." Her tone filled me with sadness as if she were crying, "Woe is me."

The only change I could see was that Ernest was more dashing and handsome. Arm-in-arm with the two sisters and Bert, he and his fiancée swung down the hill to the park where the annual Band of Hope Demonstration was in full swing with all the brass bands of the town which was *en fête*. Gaily they marched in the sunshine, all brimming over with joy of life. I suddenly felt grieved to think of the mother alone at home looking out on the gloomy back yard, apart from the fun and laughter that they made.

But the next time I saw Mrs. Lawrence, she was in a fury and began talking:

"They're gone! Aye, they're gone, and I for one am not sorry. Why, child, she lets him buy her boots!"

The tirade continued. Bert had heard it before and stood patiently waiting till he could go down the entry with me and said:

"I don't think it matters, do you?"

I didn't know. Such a torrent shrivelled me and left me dazed. I said it must matter, or his mother wouldn't be so angry.

"I don't think it does," Bert said. "They're sweethearts. If they give presents, they can just as well be useful. They were very pretty boots. He paid— Guess how much he paid for them . . . ." And he named a sum that filled us with awe. "But I don't think it matters, she's his sweetheart."

I thought his mother knew best, but Bert stuck to his own opinion. . . .

Since Mother refused to have Bert bring food [to the Haggs], I was invited to tea at his home in his holidays. He had been on some errand and met me as I came from school. We looked into the confectioner's.

"What would you like?" Bert asked.

I said, "Some of everything," and he turned away with a laugh.

"Well, you won't get any, not even a tantafflin. We don't have them till Sunday, so come thy ways."

This banter and laughter continued till we all sat down to the table. Bert and I sat on the sofa; and when his father took his place, I felt Bert draw himself together, humping himself up and bending his head over his plate. When the father talked to me, the son twitched my dress or nudged me. He hardly answered when his father spoke to him. His mother kept her eyes down and spoke only in monosyllables. But the father talked, and ate and handled the food as the man who paid for it all. He chatted amiably with me, and his young daughter [Ada] told of some prank that made us laugh. But his son nudged me so hard I felt I was misbehaving. There was such a hateful feeling coming from Bert that I was almost frightened. It was as if Prince Charming had changed into a toad.

The father went out when the meal was over, and Mrs. Lawrence said:

"He hates his father. That little minx will sit on his knee, but not the boy. He keeps his distance, he never goes near him if he can help it. He hates his father."

Bert's gaiety returned as his father's steps echoed in the entry; and when a couple of neighbour girls came in, he was sparkling with

them. He seemed to be very happy to be the only man in a houseful
of women, or rather girls, for his mother joined in the banter, en-
riching it like a dash of spice with iron caustic wit. After a noisy burst
of hilarity, I thought how different it would be if a father wanted to
sit quietly reading his newspaper, and I asked:

"Does Mr. Lawrence go out every night?"

"While his money lasts," said his wife, grimly.

"Oh, but then he goes to bed," put in one of the girls quickly, as if
to assure me we need fear no intrusion of the father's presence.

Next time Bert was at our tea table, I offered him the cream.

"You know Bert doesn't take cream," remarked Mother.

But I pressed it on him till he said:

"I don't like it, I like the taste of the tea."

And I informed my family, "Those are the very words his father
used when I passed him the cream jug!"

Bert reddened. "Yes, he doesn't take it."

And I followed up: "Fancy you inheriting his taste!" For I couldn't
forget the waves of hate that came from him as he humped himself up.

One of us always went as far as the Warren with Bert, and I seemed
to be the only one not reading when he was ready to start. So I went,
and carried a couple of books with a string around them. The string
was twisted around my finger as I passed them to him. He steadied my
hand as he spun the books to unwind the string, then dashed away my
books spitefully.

"Goodnight," he said laughingly.

"Goodnight, prince into a toad!" I returned.

But he was running and did not turn to answer me. . . .

A few days later, I had tea again at Bert's home. The father had
come from the pit and ate heartily of his dinner of meat and vegetables,
ignoring the attitude of his wife and son who sat next me on the sofa,
humped up and uncivil. The father talked of his work and of my
grandmother, and listened indulgently to his little daughter [Ada]. I
tried to find a word to fit Bert's attitude and discovered it was *venge-
ful.* He was totally unlike the boy who lit up the rather drab room
with a dancing light like a sunbeam. He seemed to gather the gloom of
the back yard into his being and crouch among the shabbiness like
something sinister. The wooden chairs, the well-worn sofa, the dresser
with the ill-fitting drawers showed only honest wear and tear of years of
service, but Bert seemed to send out jagged waves of hate and loathing
that made me shudder. The father was hungry after his day's work in
the pit and ate heartily as he talked—evidently so used to the atmosphere of animosity that he did not feel it. I wanted to get away. The
queer behaviour of mother and son made me tremble internally till
I couldn't swallow my food. The mother poured us more tea, and her
husband drank thirstily.

"I was dry," he said to me. "You like milk in your tea? You should try it wi'out. You'd soon get used to it, then you'd like it better. You get the taste of the tea. Milk just spoils the taste of the tea. You just try wi'out."

He rose from the table and bade me "Come and see us again before long," and went out immediately.

As his step echoed in the entry, his son shed his malignancy. . . .

Then tragedy struck. Ernest, the auburn-haired brother, was so ill in London that his parents had been sent for. He had paid a flying visit home at Goose Fair, and had seemed abounding with life. I had seen his dazzling smile with a touch of the audacious which added to his attraction. Now he was at death's door.

On a Saturday night in October [1901], I was at the Station to meet a friend of Mother's standing as arranged under the one lamp. The train came in, the carriage doors flew open; but in the stream of passengers I saw only one figure, short, black, bowed, but tearless, stunned with grief but wearily attending the work of the movement. Her husband followed heavily behind as she went to attend to the coffin's transfer. Her face looked shrunken under the small bonnet; grief and pain seemed concentrated in the pitiful eyes.

My mother's friend was kissing me under the lamp, but all I could say was, "Look at poor Mrs. Lawrence, she's brought Ern home in his coffin!" The night was very black, and the city friend complained bitterly of dark, country roads. But the blackness seemed in keeping with my thoughts of Ern in his coffin and the family grieving—and now for evermore a sadness in our lives like a black band running through bright colours. . . .

Since Bert was recuperating [from pneumonia], he spent much time at our farm, the walk back and forth thought to be beneficial. He roamed the fields with these two young brothers; and when they spotted the first mushrooms, his long legs carried him to them first, and he pocketed them, to the disgust of the young boys, who argued:

"They are on our land—they're ours."

"Findings' keepings," Bert retorted hotly.

"You didn't find 'em. It's just cos you've got such long legs. They're ours on our land."

"They're wild, and wild things are free for him who's sharp enough to get them."

"Well, I don't reckon to be as sharp as you, but I spread salt to make them grow, and so you're stealing them."

They brought the dispute home, and Bert was allowed to keep them.

"All that fuss," he said to me angrily, "over four or five mushrooms, a measly few like that! Be different if it was a score."

"Yes, why did you make such a fuss?" I asked.

He threw up his head defiantly.

"I found them, and they're wild, salt or no salt."

I shook my head.

"Well, if you want to know, I want them for my father's tea," he announced.

"Well!" I cried in sheer surprise, "and you hating him as you hate him! You don't hate him as you pretend you do, or you'd never make trouble with your friends to take their mushrooms for him!"

"I have to hate him for Mother's sake," he replied. "But I can take mushrooms home when I find them, and they'll be for his tea because he loves wild things you find. I hope you're satisfied, now you know!". . .

Bert's little band of followers was enlarged, and his home of an evening was lively with several girls and a boy or two come for help from D. H. L., who sat at the table hammering something into one or another, or studying while they and his family larked. His concentration was a marvel to us. Suddenly he would look up and take part in the general conservation of which his mother was the centre.

"The women say I shall never get old mixing like this with the young ones," Mrs. Lawrence beamed.

And Bert observed indulgently:

"The little woman fancies herself among the lads and lasses. It is rather flattering, isn't it, Lyddy?" (Her name was Lydia.)

There were derisive cries of "Oh, Dickie!" for Bert would not acknowledge his third name Richard from us. His mother vigorously applauded.

How different a mother and son from when the father was present! She liked the attention of the little group, and he liked playing host. Her caustic wit and positive advice drew the young people who delighted in their young host instead of an elderly father who might have scowled on their intrusion. The mother was a different woman from the complaining housewife of the mornings. The banter of the young folk stimulated her, and their inexperience of life brought out her most emphatic statements and her opinion of people, so that to them she sounded very wise and absolutely sure of herself. And at the back of all was pity that she had a husband who spent his evenings in public houses. We spoke with bated breath of the story she told some of us of being put out one night before one of her children was born.

"He put me out and locked the door," she said in bitter remembrance of the night she spent in an outhouse. "Aye, there's a reason for hate and nasty temper. It was in them before they were born."

Some of the group were so impressed that it seemed a duty to stand up for Mrs. Lawrence against the divided sympathy found among the older generation. . . .

Soon after this, Bert happened to find me alone in the kitchen and, sitting down quickly, said:

"I say, what are we?"

"If you mean what do our parents think we are—we seem to be their possessions."

"You're right," he said vehemently. "Mothers are too possessive."

"Some parents think we belong to them, never to ourselves," I went on. "And I think I belong to myself, don't you?"

Bert looked dejected and wounded; but, someone coming in at that moment, the subject was changed. . . .

Bert had come home "to wait—," as he said.

"[Mother] doesn't want to die."

"No," I said. "How do you comfort her?"

"I can't, but my sisters do. They say, 'You'll see Ern and Grandmother, and all you have missed so much.' But she says, 'I've learned to do without them. I want to stay with those I have here.' And they tell her again how nice it will be to see them in heaven, and how we shall come to her. They can make believe like that, but I can't, I can't. I've nothing to offer her. No comfort at all."

He sat shaking his head slowly, sorrowfully, looking disconsolate.

"Well, she saw [your *White Peacock*]," I offered. "It must comfort you to have achieved that while she could have pride in it."

But he was shaking his head.

"No, no," he said sadly.

"No?" I echoed.

"No, she didn't like it."

"Why?" I demanded.

He shook his head sadly.

"I don't know. She didn't like it. Even disliked it."

"Still," I protested, "she must be proud of you, of your ability to write a book. You've given her that. It can't help but be a source of pride."

"No," he insisted miserably, "she doesn't like what I write. Perhaps if it had been romance . . . . But I couldn't write that."

He had sat with his hands clasped loosely between his knees, his head bent. Now he glanced up at me with a piteous smile.

"Strange, isn't it, that I couldn't please her?"

I shook my head.

"What *did* she want?"

"Me," he said softly. "Just me."

"Death long drawn out is an awful thing," Bert said one day, trying to smile.

"It shouldn't be allowed, really," he said presently, and his voice was rough as if his throat ached. For a long time he sat looking into the fire.

"There Mother lies all day, almost silent."

"And you just watch and wait," I said.

"Just watch and wait," he echoed softly.

After a while he repeated it.

"Just watch and wait, watch and wait. There's nothing more to do. She doesn't talk to us at all now. She hardly speaks. She's hardly conscious and yet," he paused and looked at me, "at the exact right time she says, 'Have they got your father's dinner all ready for when he comes home?'" His eyes and voice were soft and questioning. "Why does she think of that? How does she know the time? If either of the girls is there, she asks, 'Is your father's dinner ready?' It's all she can do to say as much as that, and yet she makes the effort. Why is it? Is it mere habit, the habit of thirty-odd years? Or is it that she regrets, or recalls . . . ?"

His voice trailed off into silence as he looked into the fire.

"She's barely conscious now. I doubt if she knows us."

Bert pressed his back against the high armchair and lifted his head as if bracing himself to say it:

"And Father never goes up to see her."

I said, "But he asks."

"Oh, he asks. Every day as he gets in from the pit, he asks, 'How's your mother today?' and we tell him." His voice fell to a shocked, almost horrified tone. "But he never goes up to see her."

"He knows without seeing," I said.

"But he *ought* to go up," he insisted softly. "He ought to *want* to see her. He should go up."

"He can't," I ventured. "Things have happened between them."

"But he was once her lover," he protested with wide eyes.

"That doesn't matter," I said.

"Then what does matter?" he demanded in a voice that broke as if strangled. . . .

A day or two later [9 December 1910], Bert came in with a hurt and tender expression on his face.

"She's gone," I said.

He nodded. "It's all over." He turned as the door opened. "Mother died this morning, Bill."

"Your mother's dead, eh?"

"Mother is dead," he repeated.

We all stood looking, asking with our eyes the questions that were tearing at our hearts. What is death? Where is she now? Oh, where is she now?

Suddenly I said:

"Let us help you. Can we help you? Is there *anything* we can do?"

Then we all sat down to discuss immediate plans. Bill was to drive to the station for the flowers on the day of the funeral.

"I shall write little poems to her," Bert said. "She'd like that."

Chronology of Important Dates

	D. H. Lawrence	Historical Events
1885	D. H. Lawrence born on September 11 in Eastwood, Nottinghamshire, England.	Tennyson, *Tiresias.*
1888		Death of Matthew Arnold. Birth of T. S. Eliot.
1895		Yeats, *Poems.*
1901	Leaves Nottingham High School. Clerks at Haywood's factory. Meets Jessie Chambers. Develops pneumonia after brother Ernest dies.	Death of Queen Victoria. Thomas Mann, *Buddenbrooks.*
1905	After attending Nottingham University teaches school in Croydon.	Einstein develops theory of relativity. Freud, *Drei Abhandlungen zur Sexualtheorie.*
1909	Publishes first poems in *The English Review* under title, "A Still Afternoon."	Death of George Meredith.
1910	Lawrence's mother dies. He begins *Paul Morel* (*Sons and Lovers*).	Marie Curie, *Traité de radioactivité.*
1912	Meets and elopes with Frieda Weekley.	Thomas Hardy, *The Wessex Novels* (revised text, through 1931).
1913	Publishes *Sons and Lovers* (May 29) and *Love Poems.*	Proust, *Du Côté de chez Swann.* Stravinsky, *Le Sacre du Printemps.* Frost, *A Boy's Will.*
1915	*The Rainbow* published, declared obscene; copies seized in London.	Conrad, *Victory.*

1916	Publishes *Amores; Twilight in Italy.*	Joyce, *Portrait of the Artist as a Young Man.* Pound, *Lustra.*
1920	Publishes *Women in Love* privately in New York.	Fitzgerald, *This Side of Paradise.* Lewis, *Main Street.*
1922	Publishes *Aaron's Rod; Fantasia of the Unconscious.* Settles at Mabel Luhan's ranch in Taos, New Mexico.	Joyce, *Ulysses.* Eliot, *The Waste Land.* Housman, *Last Poems.*
1923	Publishes *Kangaroo; Birds, Beasts and Flowers; Studies in Classic American Literature.* Pays Mrs. Luhan for his home, Kiowa Ranch, with *Sons and Lovers* manuscript.	Rilke, *Duineser Elegies.* Stevens, *Harmonium.*
1925	Publishes *St. Mawr; Reflections on the Death of a Porcupine.* Lawrence, suffering tubercular attacks, returns with Frieda to Italy.	Kafka, *Der Prozess.* H. D., *Collected Poems.*
1928	Publishes *Lady Chatterley's Lover,* of which Yeats writes that its "forlorn poetry" is "something ancient, humble and terrible. . . ."	Huxley, *Point Counter Point.*
1929	*The Escaped Cock; Pornography and Obscenity* published. London police confiscate 13 Lawrence paintings at the Warren gallery. *Pansies* (poems) and copies of *Lady Chatterley* destroyed in London.	Faulkner, *The Sound and the Fury.*
1930	Lawrence dies in a Vence sanatorium, March 2.	Crane, *The Bridge.*
1932	*Last Poems; Etruscan Places; Letters* published.	

Notes on the Editor and Contributors

JUDITH FARR has taught at Vassar College and is Assistant Professor of English at the State University of New York, New Paltz. She has written criticism, short stories, and poems for *American Literature, The Minnesota Review,* the *Riverside Anthology,* and other periodicals and is preparing a collection of short stories and a study of Lawrence.

GEORGE H. FORD, Joseph H. Gilmore Professor of English at the University of Rochester, is the author of *Keats and the Victorians, Dickens and His Readers,* and *Double Measure: A Study of the Novels and Stories of D. H. Lawrence.*

EDWARD GARNETT, English critic, biographer, and essayist, publisher and friend of D. H. Lawrence, wrote *Friday Nights, Hogarth, Turgenev,* and studies of Robert Frost and numerous other contemporary authors.

ALFRED KAZIN is Distinguished Professor of English at the State University of New York, Stony Brook. He has written *On Native Ground, A Walker in the City,* and *Starting Out in the Thirties.*

(PERCY) WYNDHAM LEWIS, American-born English novelist, painter, and essayist, was the leader of a school of painting called Vorticism, and the author of several books, among them *Apes of God.*

KARL MENNINGER, founder of the Menninger Clinic, wrote *The Human Mind, Man Against Himself,* and *Love Against Hate.*

FRANK O'CONNOR (MICHAEL O'DONOVAN), Irish writer and critic, wrote numerous short stories, collected as *Bones of Contention, The Common Chord,* and others; and critical studies, *The Lonely Voice* and *The Mirror in the Roadway.*

KEITH SAGAR is Staff-Tutor in the Extra-Mural Department of the University of Manchester and the author of *The Art of D. H. Lawrence.*

MARK SCHORER, critic and novelist, is Professor of English at the University of California, Berkeley, and the author, among other books, of *The Wars of Love, Sinclair Lewis: An American Life,* and *The World We Imagine.*

ERNEST SEILLIÈRE (BARON ERNEST ANTOINE AIMÉ SEILLIÈRE) wrote *Le mal romantique, Marcel Proust,* and various studies of French and English romanticism.

MARK SPILKA is Professor of English at Brown University. His works include *The Love Ethic of D. H. Lawrence, Dickens and Kafka: A Mutual Interpretation,* and *Twentieth Century Views of D. H. Lawrence.*

FATHER WILLIAM TIVERTON (MARTIN JARRETT-KERR), an Anglican priest, wrote *D. H. Lawrence and Human Existence.*

DANIEL A. WEISS, who is Associate Professor of English at San Francisco State College, wrote *Oedipus in Nottingham: D. H. Lawrence.*

KINGSLEY WIDMER, Professor of English at San Diego State College, has written *The Art of Perversity: The Shorter Fictions of D. H. Lawrence* and *The Art of Perplexity: Melville's Novellas.*

VIRGINIA WOOLF, distinguished English novelist, critic, and member of the Bloomsbury Group, was, with her husband, Leonard Woolf, co-founder of the Hogarth Press and the author, among other books, of *Mrs. Dalloway, To the Lighthouse, The Waves,* and the first (and *Second) Common Reader.*

Selected Bibliography

Text and Background Materials

The manuscript of *Sons and Lovers* in its uncut form is now at the Library of the University of California at Berkeley, but may not be seen prior to its intended publication at some future date. E. W. Tedlock, Jr., was permitted to see it a few years ago and gives a brief account of some differences between the manuscript and the published version of the novel in his *D. H. Lawrence and "Sons and Lovers," Sources and Criticism* (New York: New York University Press, 1965), pp. 66–69.

Chambers, Jessie ("E. T."). *D. H. Lawrence, A Personal Record*. London: Jonathan Cape, Ltd., 1935. The famous account of her friendship with the young Lawrence and of the writing of *Sons and Lovers*.

Corke, Helen. *D. H. Lawrence, The Croydon Years*. Austin, Texas: The University of Texas Press, 1965. A description of the composition of *Sons and Lovers* and of its consequences for Lawrence's friends.

Lawrence, Ada and G. Stuart Gelder. *Young Lorenzo, Early Life of D. H. Lawrence*. New York: Russell and Russell, 1966. Reminiscences of the Lawrence home and of Lawrence as a boy, together with a lecture on the purposes of art given by Lawrence when a youthful schoolmaster.

Lawrence, D. H. *Phoenix*, ed. Edward McDonald. New York: The Viking Press, 1936. *Phoenix II*, ed. Warren Roberts and Harry T. Moore. New York: The Viking Press, 1968. "Nottingham and the Mining Countryside" (I) and "On Coming Home," "Return to Bestwood," and two "Autobiographical Sketch[es]" (II) provide Lawrence's impressions of his town and early life.

Lawrence, Frieda. *Not I, But the Wind*. New York: The Viking Press, 1934. Mrs. Lawrence's memoirs and her description of the last stages of the writing of *Sons and Lovers*.

Moore, Harry T. *The Intelligent Heart*. New York: Farrar, Straus and Young, 1954. A full and readable account of Lawrence's life.

Nehls, Edward. *D. H. Lawrence, A Composite Biography*, Vols. I–III. Madison: The University of Wisconsin Press, 1957–59. An invaluable compendium of recollections and judgments of Lawrence, with excerpts from his and others' letters and essays. Volume I provides a rich study of the *Sons and Lovers* period; Volume III contains the Chambers papers with their vivid account of Lawrence's early years.

Roberts, Warren. *A Bibliography of D. H. Lawrence*. London: R. Hart-Davis, 1963. Replaces the *Bibliography of D. H. Lawrence* (Philadelphia, 1925) and *Supplement* (1931) compiled by Edward McDonald with respect to its descriptions of the various printings of *Sons and Lovers*.

Critical Books

Readers should refer to the fuller original texts of many of the essays reprinted in this volume. In addition, the following may prove useful:

Daleski, H. M. *The Forked Flame, A Study of D. H. Lawrence*. Evanston: Northwestern University Press, 1965. Explores Lawrence's treatment of Gertrude and Walter Morel.

Hough, Graham. *The Dark Sun, A Study of D. H. Lawrence*. New York: Macmillan, 1957. An acute discussion of the Miriam chapters as the core of *Sons and Lovers*.

Moore, Harry T. *The Life and Works of D. H. Lawrence*. New York: Twayne Publishers, 1951. The chapter "The Genesis [of *Sons and Lovers*] as Revealed in the Miriam Papers" provides a detailed description of the *Paul Morel* manuscripts and analyzes the extent of Jessie Chambers' contributions to these early versions of *Sons and Lovers*.

Moynahan, Julian. *The Deed of Life, The Novels and Tales of D. H. Lawrence*. Princeton: Princeton University Press, 1963. Analyzes the "three formal orders" of *Sons and Lovers*: "autobiographical narrative," the psychoanalytic "matrix," and the "matrix of 'life.'"

Murry, John Middleton. *Son of Woman*. New York: J. Cape and H. Smith, 1931. A study of the author (and qualities) of *Sons and Lovers* by Lawrence's friend, enemy, and rival.

Critical Articles

Betsky, Seymour. "Rhythm and Theme: D. H. Lawrence's *Sons and Lovers*," in *The Achievement of D. H. Lawrence,* ed. Harry T. Moore and Frederick J. Hoffman. Norman, Oklahoma: University of Oklahoma Press, 1953. Characterizes the novel as "a self-purgation" and examines the formal issue of "how much of [it] is successfully realized."

Lindenberger, Herbert. "Lawrence and the Romantic Tradition," in *A D. H. Lawrence Miscellany,* ed. Harry T. Moore. Carbondale, Illinois: Southern Illinois University Press, 1959. A brief treatment of *Sons and Lovers* as part of a romantic fictive tradition founded in *The Prelude*.

Van Ghent, Dorothy. "On Sons and Lovers," in *The English Novel: Form and Function*. New York: Holt, Rinehart, and Winston, Inc., 1953. A discussion of the "poetic logic" of the book.